ROTO ... HIC

Specialist publishers of price guide reference books. Established 1959

British and Irish Campaign medals, 1899 to 2006.

By Stephen Philip Perkins
(Member of the Orders and Medals research society)

1st Edition © 2006

ISBN: 0-948964-75-8

A wealth of information about British and Irish campaign medals from the second Boer War to modern times. With a compilation of averaged sell-ing-prices drawn from dealers' lists, auctions, magazines and experience n the medal trade.

Most of the images in this book are of medals in the author's own collection. Thanks are due to Chelsea Military Antiques (see advert on page 65), Mr D Hann of Pembrokeshire (derrickhann41@aol.com) and Tony Cooper of EG Frames in Tamworth (www.egframes.co.uk) for the loan of many quality medals and replica medals which were used to provide some of the images of rarer types. Most of the medal Images in the Irish section were provided by Peter Sheen of Dublin (www.military-medals-online.com - see also the advert on page 93).

Errors and Omissions:

Every effort has been made to ensure that the information and price data contained within this book is accurate and complete. However, errors do sometimes creep in unnoticed, and with this in mind the following email address has been established for notifications of omissions and errors: omissions@rotographic.co.uk. Readers within the UK can also call the telephone number below.

www.rotographic.co.uk
0871 871 5122

In Association with Predecimal

A Dedication

This small volume is dedicated to all the ordinary men and women who have done extraordinary deeds in Great Britain and Ireland's time of need in the conflicts and wars of the previous 107 years, whatever the political implications. All of us today owe a debt of gratitude to these brave and loyal individuals.

A special dedication to my late father George Henry Perkins who served with the Royal Marines Light Infantry Division during and after the First World War. And to my brother, William George Perkins, who also served in the Royal Marines but was tragically killed, aged 19, on the morning of 21st May 1941 when his ship HMS Hood was blown apart in seconds by enemy gunfire (www.hmshood.com for more information).

To Edward Briggs, the last living survivor from the HMS Hood crew, who I had the pleasure to meet in 2001 and to the HMS Hood Association.

And to all members and associate members of the Royal British Legion who do so much unsung work for ex-servicemen and their families.

Finally to my son, Chris Henry Perkins, without whose encouragement this book would not have been written, and without his amateur photography skills, would not contain illustrations!

Stephen Philip Perkins

William George Perkins and HMS Hood, the ship on which he lost his life. William was posthumously awarded the 1939 - 1945 Star (page 35), the Atlantic Star (page 37), the Africa Star (page 42) and of course, the War Medal (page 56).

George Henry Perkins during WWI

Contents

Introduction

Collecting campaign medals is a fascinating hobby. In this year of the 92nd anniversary of the beginning of The First World War and the 62nd anniversary of the D-Day Landings many of us will know of a relative who served in either (or both!) of these major conflicts of the 20th century. The awards that our fathers, grandfathers or great grandfathers received are not only part of the Nation's heritage but they are part of individual family history. Many collectors start by tracing their own relative's medal awards and then the interest in the subject takes them into other areas. For example, some collectors will specialise in a particular conflict or branch of service, others will research in detail the recipient's service history. Collecting campaign medals is many things to different people; history, geography, genealogy, research, etc. It can also be an excellent teaching aid for children taking history at school.

Whatever your reason for collecting I hope you find this little book informative and useful.

What exactly are Campaign Medals?

Campaign medals are awarded to members of the armed services and occasionally members of civil institutions for taking part in a campaign or service in time of war. Clasps are often added to the medal for taking part in a particular action or battle within that campaign, e.g. the 2nd World War, Africa Campaign, clasp - "NORTH AFRICA 1942 - 43", awarded to servicemen who served in Africa, or in African waters.

Starting your collection

As mentioned above, many people start their collection with their own family's awards, but there are many other places to find medals.

Militaria Collectors' Fairs – are a very good source. These fairs are very popular. You can purchase anything from a Napoleonic cavalry officer's sword to a German SS uniform. You will usually find many dealers at these fairs, so there is much to choose from. If you are paying cash always haggle for the best price. These fairs are usually advertised in the local press along with other collector's fairs.

Second Hand Shops/Antique Shops – Many of these shops will have a small selection of medals on display. As with fairs always haggle for the best price.

Auctions – You can often pick up bargains at auctions. There are many small auction houses up and down the country. You don't have to attend every auction – just subscribe to their catalogue where all the lots will be listed with their reserve/start prices. Details of payment, collection etc. will also be in the catalogue.

Dealers – Specialist dealers will have a good selection at current prices. Most dealers are a good source of advice. You will normally have to pay the asking price. If you become a regular customer ask for a discount!

The Internet – You can do all the above without leaving the comfort of your own home, but you won't be able to talk to people face to face with the same interests, and as with any form of anonymous trading, you have to try to check out the credentials of any sellers as best as possible before parting with cash.

THE BOER WAR 1899- 1902

Background:

The Boer War was fought in what is now South Africa, between British/Imperial Troops, (South African, Indian, Australian and New Zealanders) and the Afrikaners or 'Boers'.

In 1836 the majority of Boer farmers moved northward from the Cape Colony to settle in the Orange Free State, Transvaal and Natal due to the failure of the British to compensate them enough for the abolition of slavery in the British Empire in 1833. The Boer journey to the new territory was known as the 'Great Trek'.

Under the 1852 Sand River and Bloemfontein Conventions the Transvaal and Orange Free State became independent republics, but Britain retained control of foreign policy. The Boer regions were all bordered by British annexed territory and interests.

In 1885 gold was discovered in the Transvaal. The 20,000 Boer farmers were not happy about the invasion of fortune hunters, ('uitlanders' or outsiders), who were mostly of British origin. The revenue of the Transvaal increased mainly due to the contributions and taxes to the government by the uitlanders but the outsiders were not granted full citizenship. The uitlanders appealed to Britain for support.

In 1899 there were 15,000 British troops in South Africa. On October 9th 1899 President Paul Kruger of the Tranvaal sent an ultimatum to the British authorities asking Britain to remove her troops from the Boer borders.

The ultimatum expired on the 11th October 1899 and at that time the Boer republic of the Orange Free State joined forces with the Kruger led Republic of the Transvaal. The combined strength of the Boers was now about 50,000. The Boers were perhaps not as organised as the British forces, but they were well armed, many had German manufactured weapons and some of them had been trained by mainly Dutch and German European officers.

In the latter part of 1899 the Boers invaded Natal and the Cape Colony. They besieged the towns of Ladysmith, Kimberley and Mafeking. There were then three British defeats in one week in December, (known as 'Black Week'). General Buller's army was defeated at Magersfontein, Stormberg and Colenso. From January to September 1900 reinforcements arrived from Britain led by the war heroes; Lord Roberts and Lord Kitchener. British troop numbers now reached 250,000.

The British frontal attack formations, that they had employed successfully in other colonial wars, had to change to fight the guerrilla tactics of the Boers.

Sir John French (later to be commander of the BEF sent to France in 1914) relieved Kimberley on the 15th February. Roberts and Kitchener won victories against the Boer General Cronje and the British then annexed the Orange Free State.

Ladysmith was relieved by Buller and Roberts relieved Mafeking where Colonel Baden-Powell, (founder of the Boy Scout movement), had been holding out. Baden-Powell became a national hero in Britain. From September 1900 - May 1902 the Boers carried on their competent guerrilla warfare and this caused the war to drag on much longer than was hoped by the authorities and British public. The Boer families were rounded up and put into concentration camps and Kitchener slowly trapped the remaining Boer fighters by using a system of 'block houses' and barbed wire entanglements across the country.

THE BOER WAR 1899- 1902

A peace treaty was signed at Vereeniging on 31st May 1902 and the Union of South Africa came into being in 1910. The Boer war was very different compared to previous, usually very short colonial battles, and many lessons were learnt by the British leading to overdue reforms of the Army in the run up to World War I.

THE QUEEN'S SOUTH AFRICA MEDAL

DESCRIPTION: Britannia holding the flag and laurel crown towards a large group of soldiers with warships in the background with 'SOUTH AFRICA' inscribed around the top. There were about 178,000 awarded with many variations of clasps.

OBVERSE: A veiled bust of Queen Victoria.

RIBBON: Red with two narrow blue stripes and a broad central orange stripe.

CLASPS: 26 authorised but the maximum for a single medal was 9 for the Army and 8 for the Navy.

METAL: Silver or bronze.

VALUATIONS:

British and Empire troops (Land forces)	£100 - £500
With 'RHODESIA' clasp (Royal Navy)	£1100 - £1250
With 7 clasps to Royal Marines	£1250 - £1350
With 8 clasps to Royal Marines	£1250 - £1550
Awarded to correspondents	£1150 - £1250

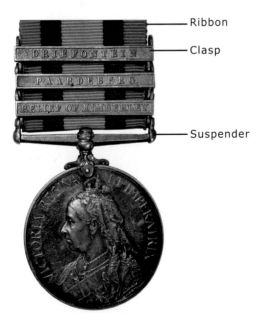

Ribbon —

Clasp —

Suspender —

The Obverse

The Reverse

THE BOER WAR 1899-1902

THE KING'S SOUTH AFRICA MEDAL 1901-1902

DESCRIPTION: Similar to the Queen's South Africa medal. The obverse now features the bust of Edward VII in uniform.

RIBBON: Three equal stripes of green, white and orange

CLASPS: "SOUTH AFRICA 1901" and "SOUTH AFRICA 1902"

METAL: Silver.

VALUATIONS:

To Royal Navy with 1901/1902 clasps	£825 - £1550
To New Zealand troops	£350 - £400
Issued to Nurses (no clasp)	£225 - £300
1901/1902 British army	£70 - £80
1901/1902 (Canadian)	£85 - £110
1901/1902 (Australian)	£110 - £160
1901/1902 (South African troops)	£65 - £85
1902 clasp	£110 - £160

QUEEN'S MEDITERRANEAN MEDAL 1899 – 1902

Awarded to officers and men of the Militia who were sent to fill gaps and reinforce the Mediterranean garrisons in Malta and Gibraltar while the regular troops went to fight in South Africa. Similar in design again to the Queen's and King's South Africa Medals.

DESCRIPTION: Obverse - Veiled Queen Victoria, as used for the Queen's South Africa Medal. Reverse - Britannia pointing, the same as the South Africa Medal but with "Mediterranean" around the edge.

RIBBON: Red with two narrow dark blue stripes and a central broad orange stripe.

METAL: Silver (5,000 awarded).

VALUATIONS: £325- £375

TRANSPORT MEDAL 1903

This medal is linked to the Boer War and the Chinese Boxer Rebellion. The medal was awarded to officers and men of the Merchant Navy who carried troops and supplies to the conflicts in South Africa and China.

DESCRIPTION: Obverse – bust of Edward VII in an admiral's uniform. Reverse shows the ship HMS Ophier below a map of the world.

RIBBON: Red with two blue stripes.

CLASPS: "SOUTH AFRICA 1899-1902" and "CHINA 1900".

METAL: Silver

VALUATIONS:

With 'SOUTH AFRICA 1899-1902'	£675 - £800 (1200 issued)
With 'CHINA 1900'	£950 - £1100 (320 issued)
With both clasps	£1250 - £1450 (178 issued)

The reverse of the transport medal - If you have this medal in your collection, please do let us know, as the editor would like to improve upon this image in the next edition.

CHINA WAR MEDAL 1900 (THE "BOXER" REBELLION)

The Boxers were a ruthless fanatical sect who were totally against the spread of Western interests in Imperial China. The term "Boxer" was a nickname given to them by the Europeans because of their original title of "The Patriotic Harmony Fists". The Boxers resented interference by Christian Missionaries and the spread of foreign trade and concessions.

Encouraged by the Chinese Royal Court, the Boxers entered Peking in June 1900. Eighty Royal Marines defended the British Legation. Other legations were defended by their own small detachments. The siege was broken after 10 weeks when the legations were relieved. German Field Marshall Count von Waldersee led the mixed nation relieving force.

DESCRIPTION: Bust of Queen Victoria on the obverse. The reverse is a trophy of arms with the Latin inscription; "ARMIS EXPOSCERE PACEM" (to pray for peace by force of arms) and "China 1900" at the bottom.

RIBBON: Crimson with yellow edges.

METAL: Silver or bronze

CLASPS: 'TAKU FORTS', 'DEFENCE OF LEGATIONS', 'RELIEF OF PEKING'.

VALUATIONS:

With the following clasp(s):

TAKU FORTS	£420 - £570 (Bronze)
DEFENCE OF LEGATIONS	£5,200 - £6,250 (Bronze)
RELIEF OF PEKIN	£230 - £295 (Bronze - Indian units only).
RELIEF OF PEKIN	£320 - £430 (Silver)
Medals with two clasps	£520 - £570
Silver with no clasps	£155 - £185
Medals to Australian Navy	£630 - £840

Illustrated over the Page...

CHINA WAR MEDAL 1900 (THE "BOXER" REBELLION)

ASHANTI MEDAL 1901

The British fought several small wars in the late 19th Century on the Gold Coast in West Africa (present day Ghana). As the name suggests, there was much mineral wealth in the area, and not only gold but also illicit slave trading. The slave trade was declared illegal in the British Empire in 1807 but it was still being carried on by the Ashanti people. In 1900 there was an uprising and the Ashanti besieged the garrison at Kumassi. This medal was awarded to the defenders and the two relieving columns (British and Native forces).

DESCRIPTION: Obverse – Edward VII, as used on the King's South Africa Medal. Reverse – A lion on a cliff looking towards the sunrise with a native shield and spears in the foreground. The word 'Ashanti' is at the bottom.

RIBBON: Black with two broad green stripes.

METAL: Silver for British soldiers, bronze to native personnel.

CLASP: "KUMASSI"

VALUATIONS:

With 'KUMASSI' clasp	£425 - £460 (silver)
Without clasp	£260 - £325 (silver) £325 - £420 (bronze)

TIBET MEDAL 1903

Described by British officer Captain George Preston at Gyantse, as a series of 'funny little fights'. Tibet 1903 was a minor campaign fought mainly by Indian troops led by British officers. The 'squabbles' started after a Trade Mission to Tibet was obstructed by local insurgents.

With superior weapons and tactics order was soon restored. At this time China had nominal control over Tibet and in 1906 Britain officially recognised China's claim. In 1911 the Tibetans rejected Chinese control and Tibet remains occupied by China to this day.

DESCRIPTION: Obverse - Bust of Edward VII. Reverse - the fortified hill town of Lhasa, 'TIBET 1903 – 4' is at the bottom.

RIBBON: Green with two white stripes and a wide maroon central stripe.

CLASPS: 'GYANTSE'.

METAL: Silver or bronze.

VALUATIONS:

Silver - British, without clasp: £400 - £525
Silver - Indian, without clasp: £275 - £310

Silver - British with "GYANTSE" clasp: £780 - £850
Silver - Indian with "GYANTSE" clasp: £325 - £425

Bronze without clasp: £120 - £130
Bronze with clasp: £260 - £350

GENERAL SERVICE MEDALS

A brief summary:

These medals were awarded for 'minor' campaigns in India and Africa. Clasps or bars were issued for various actions over a period of time.

THE AFRICA GENERAL SERVICE MEDAL

For campaigns fought in East and West Africa between 1902 – 1956. All Africa General Service Medals will be found with clasps, usually with the area and date, e.g. "EAST AFRICA 1914".

Many of these medals were awarded to personnel from The Kings Africa Rifles.

The 1920 clasp, "SOMALILAND" is in reference to the larger campaigns fought against 'The Mad Mullah'.

The most common clasp was issued in 1956 for the forces involved in the violent Mau–Mau uprising in Kenya.

DESCRIPTION: Obverse - The reigning monarch of the time from Edward VII to Elizabeth II. Reverse - A standing figure of Britannia in front of the British Lion and the word 'Africa' at the base.

CLASPS: 34 Awarded for Edward VII, 10 for George V and 1 for Elizabeth II.

RIBBON: Yellow with black edges and two thin middle green stripes.

METAL: Silver or bronze.

VALUATIONS:

CLASPS (all prices are average):

N. NIGERIA 1902 - 1906	£166
S. NIGERIA 1902 - 1906	£180
NIGERIA 1918	£140
EAST AFRICA 1910 - 1910	£220
WEST AFRICA 1906 - 1910	£240
SOMALILAND 1901 - 1920	£210

Continued on the next page...

THE AFRICA GENERAL SERVICE MEDAL

SOMALILAND 1902 - 1904	£130 - £150 RN	£130 - £155 British units	
SOMALILAND 1908 - 1910	£130 - £150 RN		
SOMALILAND 1920	£210 - £320 RN	£650- £850 RAF	
JIDBALLI (with SOMALILAND)	£210 - £260 British units		
JUBALAND	£210 - £260 RN		
GAMBIA	£650 - £850 RN		
ARO 1901- 1902	£550 - £700 British units		
KENYA	£360 - £520 RN	£90- £170 Brit	£60- £75 Afr.
KENYA	£110 - £135 RAF		

2 Clasps	£160 - £190 RN	£210 - £260 British units
2 Clasps	£160 - £260 African/Indian units	
3 Clasps	£220 - £430 African/Indian units	
4 Clasps	£320 - £470 African/Indian units	
5 Clasps	£420 - £620 African/Indian units	
6 Clasps	£750 - £1000 African/Indian units	

An Africa General Service medal with Edward VII on the obverse and clasp for **SOMALILAND 1902 - 1904.**

An India General Service medal with George V on the obverse and a clasp for **WAZIRISTAN 1925.**

THE INDIA GENERAL SERVICE MEDAL (1908 – 1935)

Most of the clasps issued for the India General Service medal were awarded for service on the North West Frontier of India. There are some exceptions:- MALABAR 1921 – 1922 and BURMA 1930 – 1932.

These two campaigns were rebellions against British rule. The first took place on the Malabar Coast in South West India (1921), and the second against the Irrawaddy in Burma (1930). These actions were mostly fought by native troops led by British officers.

The rarest India General Service Medals were awarded to RAF personnel involved in bombing raids over Waziristan in 1925.

DESCRIPTION: Obverse - Edward VII as Emperor of India (1908 – 1910). George V (1910 – 35). Reverse - Fort at Jamrud in the Khyber Pass with the word 'INDIA' in a wreath at the base.

CLASPS: 14 awarded

RIBBON: Green with broad blue central band.

METAL: Silver

VALUATIONS:

Clasp:

NORTH WEST FRONTIER 1908			
	£125 - £150 (British)		£65- £85 (Ind)
ABOR 1911 - 12	£190 - £230 (Indian)		
AFGHANISTAN N.W.F.	£75 - £110 (Brit)	£125 - £155 RAF	£40 - £60 (Ind)
MAHSUD & WAZIRISTAN 1919 - 21			
	£125 - £155 (Brit)	£155 - £190 RAF	£65 - £90 (Ind)
MALABAR 1921 - 22	£125 - £155 (Brit)		
WAZIRISTAN 1921 - 24	£65 - £100 (Brit)	£125 - £155 RAF	£40 - £60 (Ind)
WAZIRISTAN 1925		£850- £1100 RAF	
N.W. FRONTIER 1930 - 31	£75 - £100 (Brit)	£125 - £155 RAF	£40 - £60 (Ind)
BURMA 1930 - 32	£75 - £100 (Brit)		£35 - £60 (Ind)
MOHMAND 1933	£160 - £210 (Brit)	£260 - £310 RAF	£40 - £60 (Ind)
N.W. FRONTIER 1935	£75 - £100 (Brit)	£125 - £155 RAF	£40 - £60 (Ind)

THE KHEDIVE'S SUDAN MEDAL 1910

Throughout the 19th Century the British had been involved in the political and military intrigues of Egypt and the Sudan. Security in the region was essential in maintaining the 'gateway to British interests in India and the Far East' – The Suez Canal and later...oil.

In 1881 the Sudanese revolted under the leadership of Mohammed Almed – 'el Mahdi' – the chosen one, or Messiah. They drove out the Europeans and Egyptians, and General Gordon was murdered in Khartoum. Kitchener, (later to become Minister of War in 1914), re-conquered the country between 1896 and 1899.

The French tried to muscle in on the Sudan at Fashoda. They withdrew after diplomatic discussions.

After the Sudan was re-conquered the country was ruled in name only by the Khedive but to all intents it was a British protectorate.

The Khedive's Sudan Medal was awarded for actions in Southern Sudan between 1910 and 1922. These actions were fought mainly to keep the Mahdists in check.

A total of 16 bi-lingual clasps were awarded inscribed in English and Arabic.

DESCRIPTION: Obverse - 'Khedive Abbas Hilmi' and the date (all in Arabic), later changed to 'Sultan Hussein Kamil' after Abbas Hilmi was deposed in 1914. Reverse - a lion with front legs on a platform with the word 'Sudan' below with the sunrise shown in the background.

CLASPS: 16 in English and Arabic.

RIBBON: Black with thin red and green stripes on either side.

METAL: Silver, or bronze for non-combatants

VALUATIONS: From £220 without clasp, to £500 with two clasps.

WORLD WAR ONE (THE GREAT WAR - Aug 1914 to Nov 1918)

Introduction:

By 1914 Europe had become a ticking time bomb. The web of treaties and alliances bound opposing nations. France and Germany were the natural enemies, after France's humiliating defeat in the Franco-Prussian War of 1870.

In 1871 Wilhelm I of Prussia became Emperor (Kaiser) of Germany, uniting the smaller German states into the German Empire. German industry started to expand, especially in military terms, and the population increased. France, on the other hand, had a huge outdated army and her birthrate was on the decline.

Great Britain wasn't really too concerned about unfolding events on the continent but was becoming alarmed by Germany's colonial expansion, its increase in naval shipbuilding and influence in Turkish military affairs.

Europe in 1914 was a continent of empires; Czarist Russia, Germany, Austro-Hungary, Ottaman Turkey, Great Britain and Colonial France.

The spark that set Europe on fire was the assassination of Archduke Franz Ferdinand at Sarajevo in Bosnia on June 28th 1914. The heir to the Austrian throne was murdered by a small group of Serbian Nationalists, supporters of the Serbian cause.

The response from Austria was to make unreasonable demands on Serbia. Russia was allied to Serbia who was in turn allied to France. Serbia and Austria mobilised their troops; Austria then declared war on Serbia with German approval.

Through alliances and troop mobilisation Europe became two armed camps: Austro-Hungary & Germany (The Central Powers), and France, Russia and Great Britain (The Allies).

Once set in motion it was like a steam train out of control. On the 4th of August 1914, Britain declared war with Germany after the violation of the Belgian neutrality (the Germans attacked France through Belgium).

The 1914 STAR (The Mons Star)

In most peoples minds the general picture of The First World War is endless lines of opposing trenches, no-man's-land, shell craters, rows of barbed wire (a recent innovation from the USA), mud, muck and rats. The stalemate of trench warfare. However, in the early actions of 1914 there were many fast moving engagements by infantry, cavalry and artillery.

The British Expeditionary Force (BEF) was called by the German Kaiser, 'a most contemptible little army'. The BEF were highly trained regulars of the British army with years of experience of colonial warfare.

The German 'Von Schliefen plan' was to invade France through Belgium, avoiding the French fortifications along the French/German border to the south. The BEF were sent from England to support the French and Belgian armies, and the battle of Mons in Belgium was the first big engagement between British and German troops. The British were outnumbered 2 to 1, but they caused some havoc with their Lee Enfield rifles firing off 15 rounds per minute into the advancing German lines. Eventually the British were forced to retreat back to the Marne where they met up with French forces.

The battle of Mons, with the British fighting one of the most famous rearguard actions, became a legend and was celebrated in Britain as a great triumph in the early days of the war that 'would be over by Christmas'.

The 1914 Star was awarded to the British forces who served in France between the 5th of August to the 30th of November 1914. Later a bar was added to those who were 'under fire' in France or Belgium between the 5th of August and the 22nd of November 1914.

DESCRIPTION: A crowned four-pointed star with crossed swords surrounded by a wreath of oak leaves. A central scroll with the words 'Aug 1914' and the Royal cipher (GV) at the bottom.

CLASP: '5th AUG – 22nd NOV 1914'

RIBBON: Red, white and blue faded together.

METAL: Bronze

VALUATIONS: 1914 Star £70 - £90
1914 Star with clasp £95 - £150

(Illustrated on the previous page)

THE 1914 – 15 STAR

Similar in style to the 1914 Star (which was not appreciated by the 'Old Contemptibles' - the Mons veterans), but no less important. Awarded to those who served between 5th August 1914 and 31st December 1915, including those who fought the futile campaign in Gallipoli, Turkey.

Winston Churchill, now First Sea Lord, wanted to open up a second front. Russia appealed to the Allies for help in the Black Sea area now that Turkey had joined the war on the Central Powers' side. A plan began to materialize in London. It was decided to hit at Turkey through the Dardanelle's Straits and capture Constantinople, hopefully this would lead to Turkish surrender.

It was to begin with a naval bombardment by British and French ships firing on the Turkish forts and gun batteries along both sides of the narrow straits. After doing minimal damage three battleships were sunk by mines and the attack was called off.

On the 18th March 1915 there were amphibious landings on the Gallipoli Peninsula by the Allies. Then followed 8 months of heroic fighting by British, French, Australian and New Zealand forces. They fought bravely to hang on to small strips of land never getting more than a few miles inland. The Turks were a formidable enemy, always having the advantage of the high ground.

Besides fighting the Turks the Allies were fighting disease and incompetent leadership. But like Dunkirk in 1940, some good came out of the whole mess with a brilliantly executed withdrawal from December to January with only three casualties.

DESCRIPTION: As 1914 Star but with '1914 - 15' on central scroll.

VALUATIONS: £25 - £60

THE BRITISH WAR MEDAL 1914 – 1918

Six and a half million of these medals were awarded to British and Empire troops and other personnel such as nurses and support services in silver.

The vast number issued gives us some idea of the mass of people, just from Britain and The Empire, involved in The Great War. The War Medal is dated 1914-1918 but it actually covers other less well-known campaigns up to 1920.

Some of these smaller actions occurred in Russia. After the Russian Revolution in 1917 the Bolshevik government made peace with Germany. By the official end of the war in November 1918 much of Russia was still in turmoil.

The Allies (mainly Britain and France), supported the anti Communist forces, (white Russians) by sending munitions.

Some of the material was sent up to the port of Murmansk. In 1917 there was a threat of attack from Germany through Finland but after Germany's defeat the threat then came from the advancing Red Army.

Detachments of Royal Marines were sent out to secure the ports of Archangel and Murmansk. They were also involved in the securing of the 300 miles of railway between Murmansk and Kem on the White Sea. A number of Marines were trained to be ski troops and saw action against the Bolsheviks before returning to Britain in late 1919.

It is interesting to note that Sir Ernest Shackleton the famous Arctic explorer designed the Marines' winter wardrobe.

About 110,000 British War medals were awarded to non-combatants such as the Labour units, in bronze. Theses medals are now quite scarce.

DESCRIPTION: Obverse – Bare head of King George V Reverse (slightly different rendering than that used on the coinage) – St. George on horseback with the eagle shield of the central Powers underfoot and skull and cross bones. The sun rises above in Victory.

CLASPS: None issued but many proposed.

RIBBON: 'Watered' centre in orange with stripes of white, black and blue.

METAL: Silver or Bronze

VALUATIONS: British War Medal   (silver) £20- £25
                                                            (bronze) £80- £110

THE BRITISH WAR MEDAL 1914 – 1918

THE WWI VICTORY MEDAL

The allied nations each issued a version of the WWI victory medal. They are all very similar in design. Many collectors will try to obtain examples of all the allied Victory medals.

The Victory medal was awarded to all personnel who had already gained the 'Mons Star', the 1914-15 Star, and most of those who had been awarded the 1914-18 British war medal. As with the War Medal, nearly 6 million were awarded. The Victory Medal was never issued singly; it was usually awarded with the British War Medal for those who had served from 1/1/1916.

By 1917 Russia was out of the war. Germany could now move vast numbers of troops by rail from its Eastern to its Western Fronts.

The USA entered the war in 1917, although their troops were not ready for action on the Western Front. The Germans realized that there had to be one final big 'push' before the Americans were fully ready to support their allies with unlimited manpower and industrial resources.

The German spring offensives of 1918, (Operation Michael), on a 60 mile front soon had the British on the retreat. The British did not have enough reserves to back up the front line divisions.

'With their backs to the wall' (Field Marshal Haig), the British rallied and held out. Reserves were sent out from England. The Germans had over extended their lines and did not have adequate artillery cover.

British and French forces were united under the command of the French Marshal Foch. By the end of June one million American troops were on their way to Europe.

The Germans were almost a spent force and the allies were now ready to counter attack. The co-ordinated offensive with superior air cover began in July. By October the allies had broken through the heavily defended Hindenberg line. On all fronts the central powers were collapsing. General Allenby had taken Jerusalem and Damascus resulting in Turkey signing an armistice on 3rd October. The British and Italians took Austria by 3rd November.

Germany now stood alone – there was national discontent among the general public, the people were starving and there was a Naval mutiny. The Kaiser abdicated on 9th November and fled to neutral Holland. A new government came to power in Germany and signed the armistice on 11th November to end the 'war to end all wars'.

THE WWI VICTORY MEDAL

DESCRIPTION: Obverse – winged figure of 'Victory' holding a palm branch in her right hand and stretching out her left hand. Reverse – laurel wreath around the edge with the words 'THE GREAT WAR FOR CIVILISATION 1914-1919' (South African version also in Dutch below the English. The Dutch reads: 'DE GROTE OORLOG VOOR DE BESCHAVING').

CLASPS: none

RIBBON: Integrated double rainbow with indigo at the edges and red in the centre.

METAL: Bronze/brass (gold coloured)

VALUATIONS: £10- £15
£30- £40 for the rarer bi-lingual South African version.

WWI MERCANTILE MARINE WAR MEDAL

133,000 awarded – usually to be found in company with the 1914-18 British War Medal. Issued by The Board of Trade to Merchant Navy personnel who had undertaken one or more sailings through a war zone.

The Merchant seamen came under fire just as much as any soldier serving on the Western Front. Between 1914 and 1918 German submarines (U-Boats), sank over 11 million tons of Allied shipping of which 8 million tons were British.

The situation only eased when the 'convoy system' was introduced in June 1917. This system proved to be a great success – of the 16,500 ships escorted in convoys only 154 were lost.

The 'convoy' consisted of Merchant ships protected by destroyers on their flanks following a 'zig-zag' course in order to mislead enemy submarines. Over 1 Million US servicemen were brought across the Atlantic in British ships in convoys between 1917 and 1918.

DESCRIPTION: Obverse – King George V. Reverse – Merchant ship ploughing through heavy seas – sailing ship in the background. "FOR WAR SERVICE MERCANTILE MARINE 1914 – 1918" at the base.

CLASPS: None

RIBBON: Green and red with a central white stripe (green and red to indicate port and starboard navigational lights).

METAL: Bronze

VALUATIONS: £30 - £35
£160 - £200 (awarded to women)

THE TERRITORIAL FORCE WAR MEDAL 1914 - 1918

The rarest of all WWI campaign medals with just 34,000 issued. Awarded to members of the Territorial Force who had at least four years' service before the outbreak of hostilities, then had undertaken to serve overseas.

Garrison duty was enough to qualify, e.g. India, Egypt, Malta, etc. Personnel did not necessarily have to serve under enemy fire or in a 'danger zone'. The medal was awarded singly – it will usually be found with the British War Medal for non-combatants or as a trio with the British War Medal and The Victory Medal for those who saw war service.

DESCRIPTION: Obverse – Bust of King George V. Reverse – 'TERITORIAL WAR MEDAL' around the outside edge. 'FOR VOLUNTARY SERVICE OVERSEAS 1914-19' (eligibility actually ceased 11th November 1918), surrounded by a laurel wreath.

CLASPS: None

RIBBON: Yellow with two dark green stripes towards the edges combining the yellow of the old Imperial Yeomanry and the green of the Volunteer Long Service Medal

METAL: Bronze

VALUATIONS: Infantry - £125 - £160
Royal Artillery, Royal Engineers - £110 - £130
Nursing staff - £525 - £625

THE WWI MEMORIAL PLAQUE OR 'DEATH PLAQUE'

This is not a medal, but the collector will often find these plaques offered with medals and other memorabilia. The Plaque was awarded to the families of personnel killed in war service, accidents or illness, at home or abroad up until 1921. Parchment scrolls were also given with the plaque.

About 1,350,000 plaques were issued. It is not uncommon to see plaques offered with the deceaseds' service medals, obviously, all adding to the overall value. Although available, these items in groups are now becoming harder to find.

The Plaque is 120mm across in bronze with Britannia bestowing a laurel crown on to the name of the deceased on a rectangular memorial. The British Lion stands in the foreground. The inscription around the circumference reads, 'HE (or SHE), DIED FOR FREEDOM AND HONOUR'.

VALUATIONS: 'HE DIED' £45- £60
                     'SHE DIED' (rare, only 600 issued) £1200- £1650
                     Scroll - Male £25 - £35
                     Scroll - Female £750 - £1,000

Note: Canadian next of kin also received The Memorial Cross in silver, as they did in WWII

Left - The Memorial Plaque. Below - A Silver War Badge.

SILVER WAR BADGE

Along with the Memorial Plaque the Silver War Badge is another interesting item for medal collectors. First issued in September 1916 to combat the growing trend of, mainly women, presenting men of military age, not in uniform but invalided out of their fighting units, with 'white feathers' as a symbol of cowardice.

The badge carries the King's Royal Cypher in the centre. Around the edge is the legend, 'FOR KING AND EMPIRE+SERVICES RENDERED+'.
The reverse of each badge is numbered, e.g. B264844.

VALUATION: £15 - £25

GENERAL SERVICE MEDALS

The Naval General Service Medal 1915-1962

Awarded to Royal Naval and Royal Marine personnel for 'minor' conflicts between 1915-1962 for which there was no specific campaign medal.

In all there were 16 clasps awarded – some much rarer than others.

One of the most sought after Naval General Service Medals is the famous Yangtze Incident (clasp 'YANGTZE 1949'). A naval sloop, HMS. Amethyst (commanded by Lt. Cdr. J. S. Kerans), became trapped after engaging Chinese Communist forces, in the Yangtze River (April 1949). She eventually made a daring escape down 130 miles of the river in July 1949 to rejoin the fleet. There was an attempted rescue by other Royal Naval ships (The London, Black Swan and Consort). These personnel were also entitled to the award as were some RAF and Army personnel.

Another famous clasp is the 'NEAR EAST'. This clasp covers the Suez Crisis of 1956 when an attempt was made by Britain, France and Israel to seize the Canal after Colonel Nasser of Egypt had decided to nationalise the Canal. The short campaign was called Operation Musketeer and lasted from 31st October to 6th November 1956.

It was politically disastrous but militarily successful. The first helicopter assault in history - carrier-borne aircraft destroyed the Egyptian Air Force and sank Egyptian naval ships.

DESCRIPTION: Obverse – The reigning monarch of the time. Reverse – Britannia on two horses riding through the sea.

RIBBON: White with broad crimson edges and two narrow crimson stripes near the centre.

CLASPS: 16 different types, see below.

METAL: Silver

VALUATIONS:

PERSIAN GULF 1909 - 1914	
Navy (R.N) 7,127 awarded	£130 - £160
Army. 37 awarded	£575 - £875
IRAQ 1919 - 1920	£1600 - £1900
NW PERSIA 1919 - 1920. 4 awarded	Extremely Rare
PALESTINE 1936 - 1936. 13,600 awarded	£125 - £150
SE ASIA 1945 - 1946. 2000 awarded	£160 - £190
MINE SWEEPING 1945 - 1951. 4,750 awarded	£160 - £185
PALESTINE 1945 - 1948. 7,900 awarded	£125 - £130
MALAYA: George VI or Elizabeth II	£130 - £180

Continued over the page...

GENERAL SERVICE MEDALS

The Naval General Service Medal 1915-1962 (continued)

YANGTZE 1949. 1,450 awarded	£500 - £650
To HMS Amethyst crew	£1100 - £1600
BOMB AND MINE CLEARANCE 1945 - 1953. 145 awarded	£550 - £620
BOMB AND MINE CLEARANCE MEDITERRANEAN 60 awarded	£1850 - £2250
CYPRUS. 4,300 awarded	£135 - £155
NEAR EAST. 17,800 awarded	£100 - £125
ARABIAN PENINSULAR. 1,200 awarded	£220 - £260
BRUNEI. 900 awarded	£220 - £280
CANAL ZONE Oct 1951 - Oct 1954	£325 - £400

An Elizabeth II Naval General Service medal with the Canal Zone Clasp.

THE GENERAL SERVICE MEDAL 1918 - 1962

This medal was the RAF equivalent of the Naval General Service Medal. Instituted in 1923 there were 16 clasps awarded for small campaigns fought all around the world. It is common to find this medal with multiple clasps. The rarer clasps being 'SOUTHERN DESERT IRAQ' (8th Jan.- 3rd June 1928) and 'NORTHERN KURDISTAN' (15th March - 21st June 1932).

The 'PALESTINE' clasp was awarded for service during the Arab Revolt against Jewish immigration into Palestine. Security in the area was the responsibility of the British after being given the Mandate by the League of Nations in 1932. The Arabs resented the increasing number of Jewish land purchases and immigration; this led to the Arab Revolt and the troubles between 1936 - 1939. The British authorities then decided to limit the number of Jews moving into Palestine. After WWII there were more problems, hence, the 'PALESTINE 1945-1948' clasp.

The atrocities committed by the Nazis on the Jews of Europe led the survivors to unite in wanting a homeland of their own. British restrictions on Jewish immigration led to armed Jewish resistance. International support for a Jewish State resulted in Britain giving up the Mandate in 1948 and the creation of the State of Israel. Jerusalem became an international city and some 800,000 Arabs left Israel. The Jewish population, by 1948, had increased to 2.2 million heralding the Arab/Israeli problems of the present day.

DESCRIPTION: Obverse - the reigning monarch. Reverse - standing figure of Victory bestowing palms on a winged sword (symbolising the Army & RAF).

CLASPS: 18 including the most recent for 'CANAL ZONE' instituted in October 2003 for service between Oct. 1951 and Oct. 1954.
RIBBON: Purple edges with a green centre stripe.
METAL: Silver

VALUATIONS:

Clasp	British awardee	RAF	Indian/Local unit
SOUTH PERSIA (officer)	£160 - £210	N/A	£60 - £90
KURDISTAN	£90 - £110	£160 - £210	£60 - £90
IRAQ	£65 - £120	£220 - £270	£60 - £90
NORTH WEST PERSIA	£100 - £130	£260 - £320	£60 - £90
SOUTHERN DESERT IRAQ	N/A	£475 - £575	N/A
NORTHERN KURDISTAN	£360 - £460	£800 - £900	N/A
PALESTINE	£85 - £125	£65 - £100	£70 - £100
SE ASIA 1945 - 1946	£85 - £110	£85 - £110	£40 - £50
BOMB AND MINE CLEARANCE 1945-49	£400 - £425	£400 - ££425	N/A
BOMB AND MINE CLEARANCE 1945 - 56	£460 - £520	£460 - £520	N/A
PALESTINE 1945 - 48	£65 - £90	£55 - £65	£85 - £110
MALAYA (Geo VI and EII)	£65 - £85	£65 - £85	£55 - £65
CYPRUS	£65 - £85	£55 - £70	£55 - £65
NEAR EAST	£85 - £125	£85 - £125	N/A
ARABIAN PENINSULAR	£85 - £125	£65 - £85	£55 - £65
BRUNEI	£210 - 260	£190 - £230	£125 - £155
CANAL ZONE	£260 - £375	£260 - £375	N/A

Illustrated over the page...

THE GENERAL SERVICE MEDAL 1918 - 1962

THE INDIA GENERAL SERVICE MEDAL 1936-1939

Awarded to British and Indian armies and RAF personnel, covering actions fought on the North West Frontier of India between 1936 and 1939. This would be the last India General Service Medal issued because of the outbreak of WWII in 1939 and eventually the partition of India resulting in total independence in 1947.

There was difficult fighting in the Waziristan region as in the 1920's (see the I.G.S.M. 1908-35). The Islamic insurgents did not agree with the terms laid down by The Government of India Act of 1935. Many British and Indian troops had air support from the RAF based in India.

DESCRIPTION: Obverse - King George VI. Reverse - Indian Tiger with the word 'India' above. Note; Medals produced by the Royal Mint for British forces are better detailed than those produced by the Calcutta Mint.

CLASPS: 2 – 'NORTH WEST FRONTIER 1936-37' and 'NORTH WEST FRONTIER 1937-39', some examples have both clasps.
RIBBON: Central grey flanked by narrow red stripes with broader green stripes at the edges.
METAL: Silver

VALUATIONS:

NORTH WEST FRONTIER 1936-37
(British Army)   £100 - £160
NORTH WEST FRONTIER 1936-37
(RAF)   £100 - £130
NORTH WEST FRONTIER 1936-37
(Indian Army)   £40 - £50

NORTH WEST FRONTIER 1937-39
(British Army)   £100 - £155
NORTH WEST FRONTIER 1937-39
(RAF)   £90 - £130
NORTH WEST FRONTIER 1937-39
(Indian Army)   £40 - £50

With Both clasps: £160-£210 (British Army)
                    £160-£210 (RAF)
                    £55-£65 (Indian Army)

WORLD WAR II

(3rd Sep 1939 – 8th May 1945 Europe, 2nd Sep 1945 Far East)

Background:

For Great Britain the Second World War began on 3rd September 1939 when Britain, France, Australia and New Zealand declared war on Nazi Germany after Hitler's 'blitzkrieg' (lightning war) and invasion of Poland. It is often said that after WWI the Allies 'won the war but lost the peace'. After the Treaty of Versailles (1919), Germany was made to pay substantial sums in war reparations to the victorious Allied Powers. The result was Germany's economic collapse in the 1920's, out of which arose support for Adolf Hitler and the National Socialism of the Nazis.

By 1933 Hitler was the most powerful man in Germany. He could now advance his ambitious plans to dominate most of Europe. In 1939 Hitler had already had a free hand in annexing Czechoslovakia and inducting Austria into the Greater Reich. Germany had secretly built up her armed forces in the inter-war years. The German Airforce (Luftwaffe) had gained experience in Spain fighting for Franco and the Fascists (the infamous Condor Legion). Meanwhile Britain had been dis-arming with its policy of 'appeasement'.

In the Far East our ally from WWI, Japan, had already expanded into the Chinese Province of Manchuria during the 1930's fighting a bloody war much ignored by Western Governments.

December 7th 1941 saw the unexpected attack on the American Pacific fleet in Pearl Harbour in Hawaii and a simultaneous assault on Britain's valuable possession, Malaya, leading to ignominious defeat, but, it was Britain's good fortune that the USA was now at war with Japan, Germany and Italy (the Axis Powers).

In June 1941 Germany began its invasion of Soviet Russia (operation Barbarossa). Up to this time Hitler and the Russian leader, Stalin had been allies, but now Russia would enter the War on the side of the Alliance. After 6 years of deprivation Churchill and Allied leaders, Roosevelt and Stalin saw the defeat of the Axis Powers of Germany, Japan and Italy.

MEDALS & CAMPAIGN STARS OF WORLD WAR II

For WWII a series of eight 6-Pointed Stars were awarded. To save on expenditure, unlike WWI medals, these stars were usually issued un-named (with the exception of some Commonwealth countries like Australia, who named medals issued to their servicemen and women.)

The metal used was bronze, plain on the reverse with the Royal cipher of King George VI on the obverse. Around the Royal cipher is written the name of the campaign or action that the medal was awarded for.

The maximum number of stars that could be awarded to one person was five. If that person qualified for more then a clasp would be sewn on to the ribbon. Only one clasp per star was permitted. The various ribbons are said to have been designed by the King himself denoting a connection by colour to the campaign in question.

When buying medal groups from WWII always look for any documentation to determine the value of the group, for example, a researched service record.

THE 1939 - 45 STAR

Awarded for six months operational service (two months for air crews). This star usually, but not always, counted in entitlement to other campaign stars.

The actions that this medal covers are; France 1939-40 (BEF - Dunkirk), Norway 1940, Greece, Crete and various commando raids overseas.

"Never in the field of human conflict was so much owed by so many to so few" so run the words of Sir Winston Churchill. The 'Few' were the fighter pilots who fought in The Battle of Britain between July and October 1940.

After the fall of France and the Low countries Hitler's plans were now focused on the invasion of the British Isles, (code-named 'Sealion'). Before the invasion could commence the Royal Airforce had to be eliminated. Although greatly outnumbered by the Lufftwaffe the RAF had two of the best fighter aircraft of that era – the Hawker Hurricane, which entered service in 1937, and the Supermarine Spitfire which entered service in 1938. These two fighters formed the backbone of the RAF's fighter squadrons throughout the Battle of Britain and beyond. Other important factors in the British defence was the use of RADAR (RAdio Detection And Ranging) installed between 1937-39, the organisational command system championed by Air Chief Marshal Sir Hugh Dowding, Anti Aircraft Command, Balloon Command and the Observer Corps. All these key factors played a crucial role in Britain's air defences.

The Germans began the offensive in earnest by sending large formations of bombers – Junkers JU 87's (dive bombers), Heinkel He 111's, Dornier Do 17's and Junkers JU 88's, escorted by single and twin engined fighters. They first attacked 'easy' targets of shipping and coastal towns in the South and South West. Even in these early stages German losses were considerable. Around the 15th August enemy attention was focused on the RAF fighter bases in the South East, some of them, such as Biggin Hill near Bromley, were hit many times. The German bombers were no match for the fast moving Spitfires and Hurricanes, even the Messerchmitt Me 109's and Me 110's were limited in the duration that they could engage British fighters because of fuel considerations.

RAF fighter stations were struggling under the sheer bombardment from the enemy and would not be able to hold out much longer. On the 25-26th August RAF Bomber Command mounted its own raid on Berlin. In retaliation Hitler ordered the Luftwaffe to concentrate its efforts on the capital – London. This was bad news for the people of London but it was a good thing for Fighter Command who now had a 'breathing space' to re-group and to repair the airfields and aircraft.

THE 1939 - 45 STAR

On 15th September there was a massive raid by the Germans in daylight on London. 56 German aircraft were lost to 26 British. Bomber Command then struck back with a raid on what were to be Hitler's invasion barges and other craft. By 17th September operation Sealion was postponed indefinitely and Hitler turned his attention to the Russian.

After four months, what would be called The Battle of Britain ended. The cities of Britain now suffered the night raid 'blitz' but Fighter Command and all the auxiliary forces could rest assured that they had forced Hitler to call off the invasion of the British mainland.

DESCRIPTION: 6-Pointed Star, plain on the back. The obverse features the Royal cipher of King George VI. Around the Royal cipher the words 'THE 1939 - 1945 STAR'.

RIBBON: Dark blue, Red, light blue. Representing the Royal Navy, Army and Royal Airforce.

METAL: Bronze

VALUATIONS: 1939 - 45 Star £12 - £15

1939 - 45 Star with 'BATTLE OF BRITAIN' clasp £460-£550

THE ATLANTIC STAR

Awarded for service between 3rd September 1939 and 8th May 1945 for the Atlantic Campaign and service in home waters around the British Isles. Personnel had to attain six months service and entitlement to the 1939 - 45 Star before receiving this award.

The Atlantic Star was mostly awarded to Royal & Merchant Naval personnel and Royal Marines who were serving aboard HM ships. It was also awarded to Army gunners on merchant ships and RAF aircrews involved in the Battle of the Atlantic.

On the 24th May 1941 HMS Hood, the biggest and most prestigious battle cruiser in the Royal Navy was sunk in a matter of minutes by the German battle ship Bismarck.

Hood was designed at the tail end of the First World War and completed in 1920. She then spent most of the inter-war years sailing the Empire and impressing local dignitaries – a public relations exercise for the British Government. On the 18th May 1941 two German ships, Bismarck and the smaller Prinz Eugen were sent out into the Atlantic to engage British and Allied merchant shipping. As British Intelligence were aware of the two ships it was decided by the Admiralty to send as many ships as possible to find and engage the German ships before they could pose a threat to Britain's vital supplies mainly from the USA and Canada.

Although Hood and Bismarck were comparable in size and Hood had had some recent upgrades, she still lacked important deck armour. Bismarck was a masterpiece of modern German shipbuilding. In the early morning of 24th May, Hood and the new battleship HMS Prince of Wales came into action against Bismarck and Prinz Eugen in the icy waters of the Denmark Strait (between Greenland and Iceland).

Hood was on fire after an eight inch shell hit her boat deck. After more salvos from Bismarck's fifteen inch guns there was a huge explosion. Hood was blown apart and disappeared in seconds taking Admiral Holland and some 1,414 men to their watery graves. There were only three survivors.

It is thought that the Hood's magazine was hit through the vulnerable decking. The tragic loss of HMS Hood was a great blow to the morale of Royal Navy and the British public as a whole.

The Prince of Wales was damaged and retired in a trailing smoke screen, but had been lucky enough to damage Bismarck's fuel tanks and she was now losing valuable fuel oil.

Kapitän Lugens on Bismarck decided to try and lead the British into a submarine trap and then go on to reach his supply ships instead of returning to port.

Two British ships, the heavy cruisers Norfolk and Suffolk, were in pursuit of Bismarck. Prinz Eugen fled to the South. In the late evening of 24th May nine Fairy Swordfish Torpedo bombers were despatched from the carrier Victorious that was diverted from its course to Malta. The Swordfish failed to do any noticeable damage to Bismarck but the loss of fuel oil had now become critical so Bismarck now headed for the safety of the port of Brest in occupied France picking up the protection of the Luftwaffe on the way.

After a series of blunders on both sides - including Swordfish from Ark Royal attacking HMS Sheffield - Bismarck was spotted by an RAF Catalina flying boat on the 26th May.

THE ATLANTIC STAR (continued)

The faults with the topedos were remedied for the forthcoming attack on Bismarck. Two hits on Bismarck followed, resulting in the German battle ship's steering gear being severely damaged.

The following day Bismarck was surrounded by British war ships coming in to finish off the pride of the Kriegsmarine. After a lot of salvos from the British warships, Bismarck finally sank with only 110 of her crew surviving.

DESCRIPTION: A six pointed star with the Royal monogram in the centre and the words 'THE ATLANTIC STAR' below. The ribbon is watered blue, white and green representing the Atlantic Ocean.

METAL: Bronze

CLASPS: Air Crew Europe, France and Germany.

VALUATIONS: Atlantic Star £35-40, with Air Crew Europe Clasp add £30, with France and Germany clasp add £20.

THE AIR CREW EUROPE STAR

For service between 3rd September 1939 and 5th June 1944. Awarded to Air Crew that flew operational flights from the UK over Europe. The 1939-45 Star had to first be earnt before qualifying for the Air Crew Europe Star and then at least two months operational service had to be completed.

If personnel were entitled to the Atlantic or France & Germany Star then a clasp would be awarded. The Air Crew Europe Star is the rarest in the series and collectors should be made aware of fakes. However, there are some good quality replicas on the market and as long as they are sold as such, they do serve to fill a gap! Air Crew Europe Stars awarded to South Africans were named and are extremely rare.

The exploits of the air crews of Bomber Command are many and various, some have passed into legend, such as the famous "Dambusters Raid", but there are too many to go into great detail in this small volume. Suffice to say that Bomber Command was in full swing right from the very early days of September 1939 until the conclusion of hostilities. While Prime Minister Neville Chamberlain was telling the British Nation that the country was now at war with Nazi Germany an RAF Blenheim bomber was on its way to the German Naval port of Wilhelmshaven to take photos of the German fleet. Seventy-five pictures were taken of the war's first target and this was the first RAF aircraft to fly into enemy territory during WWII.

During The Battle of Britain there was a small bombing raid on Berlin that prompted Hitler to change tactics and bomb London and other cities resulting in vital breathing space for Fighter Command, which led to an advantage for the British and ultimate failure for the Luftwaffe.

Bomber Command also made a huge contribution to the Battle of Britain by sinking many of the barges that were being made ready for the proposed invasion of the British Isles.

Throughout the war German industrial targets were hit in the Ruhr, Münster and Cologne area. However, accuracy at this time was highly questionable mainly due to poor navigational aids and equipment.

In 1941 Churchill, now Prime Minister, ordered the bombing of the U-Boat bases and German shipyards. After many sorties flown there was little effect on the enemy and a loss to Bomber Command of some 300 aircraft.

New navigational equipment, including the 'Gee' pulsed transmission aid were now in preparation for the forthcoming strategic bombing offensive planned for 1942. RAF tactics were now changing to demoralise the German population by 'area' bombing.

In February 1942 Bomber Command was taken over by the dogged Air Chief Marshal Sir Arthur Harris (Bomber Harris). Morale was now very high in Bomber Command with Harris's support of area bombing. In May the RAF mounted the first 'Thousand Bomber' raid over Cologne.

To increase bombing accuracy further, 'Pathfinder' squadrons were formed. After some early disappointments these squadrons were equipped with the new Mosquito aircraft. The Mosquitoes had the new 'Oboe' navigational aid to add to their other qualities of superior speed and height.

THE AIR CREW EUROPE STAR (continued)

From early 1943 aircraft were fitted with 'H2S' a primitive ground mapping radar system. This equipment enabled aircraft to bomb through cloud. The Luftwaffe had their own breakthrough with airborne radar fitted to their night fighters. British scientists responded with a system that would confuse enemy ground radar.

May 16-17 1943 was the night of the legendary Dambusters Raid by the 617 Squadron of Lancasters equiped with the famous 'bouncing bomb' invented by Sir Barnes Wallis. The Mohne and Eder dams were breached resulting in extensive damage to the industrial Ruhr region.

More bombing raids continued over German cities, especially Hamburg, in July '43. Now there were combined attacks from the RAF at night and the American 8th Army Airforce during the day. Unfortunately many German civilians lost their lives in these raids. In August there were bombing raids over Northern Italy. The Italians surrendered on the 8th September. Other raids were carried out on Hitler's 'terror' weapons bases on the Baltic coast at Peenemünde causing delays to the V2 programme.

The Germans had now invented a device to home in on the H2S radar transmissions from British aircraft, (codenamed Naxos). Harris ordered a partial shutdown of the H2S system. By January 1944 Bomber Command losses were critical but Harris still believed that victory could only be attained by strategic bombing of German cities, especially Berlin, while the Russian Armies were advancing towards the city. From November 1943 to March 1944 587 bombers were lost – the determined German defence continued.

In preparation for the D-Day landings, Bomber Command now targeted enemy lines of communication as well as industrial targets. As June 1944 approached Bomber Command attacked the German coastal defences. The Avro Lancaster was Bomber Command's main tool, outclassing the American B17 Flying Fortress by carrying twice the bomb-load. Air Crew losses in Bomber Command were 55,000 men and 8,000 aircraft and a one in four chance of surviving a tour of 30 missions resulting in little recognition of the brave men that endured one of the most dangerous pursuits of World War II.

DESCRIPTION: A six pointed star with the Royal monogram in the centre and the words 'THE AIR CREW EUROPE STAR' below. The ribbon is Pale blue (the sky), black edges (night flying) with narrow yellow strips (enemy searchlights).

METAL: Bronze

CLASPS: Atlantic and France & Germany

VALUATIONS: Aircrew Europe Star £165 - £185.
With Atlantic Clasp add £65.
With France & Germany Clasp add £20

THE AIR CREW EUROPE STAR (continued)

THE AFRICA STAR 1940-1943

Awarded to participants in campaigns in and around North Africa between 10th June 1940 and 12th May 1943, including Abyssinia, Somaliland, Eritrea and Malta.

There were three possible clasps awarded with this Star; 'NORTH AFRICA 1942-43' for Royal Naval and Merchant Navy personnel who worked inshore and RAF personnel who flew missions over this campaign zone. '1st' and '8th ARMY' clasps were awarded for service between 23rd October 1942 and 23rd May 1943.

The North African campaign has been well documented with famous battles such as The Siege of Tobruk (April 1941), El Alamein (July 1941 for the 1st battle, and Oct 1941 for the 2nd battle) and Operation Torch (Nov 1942 - the Anglo-American landings in French North West Africa)

A lesser known incident in the North African theatre was the destruction of French Naval ships by the British at Mers-el-Kebir near Oran on the Moroccan coast. After the fall of France in June 1940 a Naval squadron had fled from the South of France to a Naval base in Morocco. The French Navy was undecided where their loyalties lay - with the Free French under De Gaulle or with the pro-German Vichy Government under the WWI hero Petain. The British, now fighting alone, did not want any French ships passing into the hands of the Germans or Italians. All French ships in British ports were forcibly taken after some confrontation with French sailors, on the 3rd July 1940.

The British Government decided that Force H (the British Naval squadron stationed in Gibraltar) would sail to Morocco to confront the French in what was to be called Operation Catapult. Force H consisted of, among other ships, the aircraft carrier HMS Ark Royal and the battle cruiser HMS Hood, commanded by Vice Admiral Somerville. The French, under the command of Vice Admiral Gensoul, were given an ultimatum to either surrender, scuttle their ships or be fired upon. Vice Admiral Gensoul, who up until now had been our ally, hesitated and after much negotiation the ultimatum ran out.

Ordered directly by Churchill the British opened fire on the French, sinking one battle ship and damaging two others. Regrettably over 1,000 of our French ex-allies were killed. Further action resulted in aircraft from Ark Royal torpedoing the damaged battle ship Dunkerque. The French Navy units at Mers-el-Kibir were now out of action and the French Naval squadron at Alexandria surrendered to the British.

DESCRIPTION: A six pointed star with the Royal monogram in the centre and the words 'THE AFRICA STAR' below. The ribbon is pale buff (desert sand), with a broad red central stripe and dark blue on the left and light blue on the right (the three services).

METAL: Bronze

CLASPS: 8th ARMY, 1st ARMY, NORTH AFRICA 1942-43

VALUATIONS: The Africa Star £15 - £20
With any of the above clasps, add £20

THE AFRICA STAR 1940-1943

THE PACIFIC STAR
8th December 1941 – 2nd September 1942

Awarded for campaigns in the huge Pacific area, including Malaya, Singapore before its defeat in Jan 1942, Hong Kong before its capture in December 1941 and actions in the Pacific during the reconquest of Japanese occupied territories.

The 1939-45 Star was not a prerequisite for Army and RAF personnel but was for the Royal and Merchant navies. Service with the Royal and Merchant navies included the Pacific and Indian Oceans and the South China Sea. Many recipients of the Pacific Star were Commonwealth soldiers who were also prisoners of war under the brutal Japanese regime.

While the air attack on Pearl Harbour raged on 7th December 1941 - eventually bringing the USA into the war - other attacks were being simultaneously co-ordinated across the Pacific. The Japanese planned offensive was to attack British, US and Dutch controlled territories at the same time.

The Japanese seemed unstoppable. December 10th saw the sinking of the British battle ship Prince of Wales and the battle cruiser Repulse. Both ships were sunk off the Malayan coast after they had been sent out to meet the Japanese threat.

On the 25th December the British Crown colony of Hong Kong surrendered along with 12,000 troops. Malaya, the star in the British Far Eastern Empire both strategically and economically, fell to the Japanese on the 15th February. The British, Malayan, Indian and Australian troops were poorly equipped and undertrained. They were no match for the Japanese who were supported by 500 aircraft and 200 tanks, (the British could only spare 150 aircraft). The main Japanese landings were on the north east coast. They quickly pushed through to the south of the country. General Percival ordered a withdrawal to Singapore Island in order to make a last stand.

There was a huge fortress on Singapore island, but it was sited in the wrong position for a landbased invasion. By the 8th February the Japanese had landed on the island and taken control of the fresh water supplies. There was no choice for the British but to surrender. It was all over by 15th February - 70,000 British and Commonwealth troops were captured - many of them would not survive and most would not survive to see the defeat of Japan by the Allies.

In May 1945, as the Americans advanced towards the Japanese mainland, Task force 58, led by four British Aircraft carriers including HMS Formidable and HMS Illustrious were sent in support. Both these ships were damaged by 'Kamikaze' attacks off Okinawa but fared better than some of the American ships with unarmoured wooden decks.

DESCRIPTION: A six pointed star with the Royal monogram in the centre and the words 'THE PACIFIC STAR' below. The ribbon is dark green (the jungle) with a central yellow stripe (the beaches), narrow stripes of dark green and light blue (Royal & Merchant navies and RAF), and wider stripes of red at the edges (the Army).

METAL: Bronze
CLASP: BURMA
VALUATIONS: The Pacific Star £35 - £40
                    With BURMA add £20

THE PACIFIC STAR
8th December 1941 – 2nd September 1942

THE BURMA STAR
11th December 1941 - 2nd September 1945

Awarded for service in the Burma Campaign, (often referred to as 'the forgotten war' by those who fought in it, because they were so far from home) and for service on land in Bengal and Assam from 1st May 1942 - 31st December 1943 and from January 1944 onwards.

The Royal and Merchant Navy awards mainly covered the Bay of Bengal. Naval personnel had to first earn the 1939-45 Star before qualifying.

Burma, once a province of British India, became nominally self-governing under British control in 1937. There had been political unrest in Burma for some years with some Nationalist Burmese (or Burmans) in communication with the Japanese before their invasion in 1942. The Burmese leader Aung San collaborated with the Japanese but the populace soon became disenchanted with the Japanese regime and supported the British in liberating their country from the Japanese.

After the initial failures by the British to stop the invasion of Burma, the Japanese, by the end of 1942, had conquered four fifths of the country cutting off overland supply to our Nationalist Chinese ally.

One of the most famous personalities of the Burma Campaign was Major General Orde Wingate who led the 'Chindit' guerrilla operations against the Japanese. The Chindits were named after the stone carved mythical creatures that stand guard over Burmese holy shrines.

Wingate was a charismatic figure who first tried deep penetration guerrilla tactics with some success in Palestine and Ethiopia. The Chindits were made up of units from the 77th Indian Infantry Brigade - approximately 3,000 men, British, Gurkha and Burmese trained to fight and survive in the harsh jungle conditions.

The first major operation was launched in February 1943 from the British base of Imphal. The Chindits had some success in disrupting Japanese lines of supply and communications. After fierce Japanese counter attacks Wingate returned with 2,000 men who were still fit for duty, and was hailed as a hero.

Encouraged by Churchill, Wingate was authorised to launch a full scale 'long range penetration offensive' under the command of Lord Mountbatten now Supreme Commander in South East Asia. In February 1944 the second major Chindit operation with 9000 men was co-ordinated as part of the Allied campaign for the reconquest of Burma. Unfortunately Wingate did not live to see the final defeat of the Japanese as he was killed in an air crash on the 24th March 1944.

DESCRIPTION: A six pointed star with the Royal monogram in the centre and the words 'THE BURMA STAR' below. Ribbon; dark blue with a wide central stripe of red flanked on either side by stripes of orange in the centre of the blue. The red represents British Commonwealth forces, the blue the Royal and Merchant Navies and the orange represents the burning sun.

METAL: Bronze

CLASPS: PACIFIC

VALUATIONS: The Burma Star   £20 - £25
With 'PACIFIC' clasp add £20

THE BURMA STAR
11th December 1941 - 2nd September 1945

THE ITALY STAR
11th June 1943 – 8th May 1945

The Italy Star covered not only the Italian Campaign but also the invasion of Pantellaria, Sicily, the Aegean, the Dodecanese, Corsica, Sardinia, Yugoslavia, South of France and Austria. It was awarded to all service and Merchant Naval personnel serving in the above locations. Commonwealth troops did not have to qualify for the 1939-45 Star first.

Mussolini, the Italian Fascist leader and disciple of Hitler, took his country to war against the Allies in June 1940. The Italian armed forces, economy and people were ill prepared for hostilities. Mussolini was only interested in gaining glory for himself on the strength of Nazi victories.

By 1943 the Italian forces were all but defeated in numbers and fighting spirit. There had been disastrous actions in Egypt, Greece, East Africa and the Western Desert. In 1943 the Germans and Italians had been driven out of North Africa. Preparations by the Allies now began for the invasion of Sicily and the Italian mainland, referred to by Churchill as 'the soft underbelly of Europe' – he could not have been more wrong.

After the successful invasion of Sicily by British and American forces, conspirators moved quickly to replace Mussolini with a new head of government, Marshal Badoglio. Peace feelers were then put out to the Allies. Mussolini was briefly under arrest but was rescued in a daring raid by German Airborne troops and taken to his friend Hitler in Germany. Mussolini was later given control of the German occupied northern region of Italy based at Lake Garda.

The Italian government accepted an armistice on 1st September 1943 but the German forces in Italy would fight on. British veterans of the North African Campaign, the 8th Army, landed on the 'toe' of Italy at Reggio. On the 9th September the American 5th Army then made an amphibious landing north west of Reggio. Other landings and air attacks followed. The Allies gradually clawed their hard fought way to the infamous 'Gustav Line'.

The Gustav Line ran from east to west roughly half way up the Italian peninsula. It was fortified with concrete bunkers, machine gun emplacements and minefields centred around the hilltop monastery of Monte Cassino. The line was held by some 15 German divisions under the command of Field Marshal Kesselring.

There followed some of the bitterest fighting of the Italian Campaign involving a joint Allied offensive by British, US, New Zealand, French, Polish and Indian troops. The first attempts to take Cassino began in January by the Americans followed by the New Zealanders in February and then the 4th Indian Division in March. All these attacks failed to dislodge the elite German Parachute troops from the defences around the 6th century monastery.

While Monte Cassino was being attacked there was an outflanking amphibious landing at Anzio, 60 miles to the north. The American met little resistance with their surprise landings but were soon delayed while waiting for vital equipment. At this time priorities for equipment, supplies and manpower were now going to Britain in preparation for the proposed invasion of the French coast - Operation Overlord. The delay gave the Germans vital time to reorganise their defences. From March to May there was stalemate at Anzio. On the 23rd May there was a combined British and US breakout from Anzio resulting in many casualties for both sides.

THE ITALY STAR
11th June 1943 – 8th May 1945

A controversial decision was made to bomb the Monte Cassino Monastery in the February. The massive bombardment and resulting destruction only gave the Germans more defendable positions. The breakthrough at Cassino came in mid May with a concerted effort by Polish and French forces. With the combined successes at Cassino and Anzio came the Allied advance to Rome itself itself which was liberated the day before 'D-Day' - the 5th June 1944.

As the Gustav line broke the Germans now retreated further north to the 'Gothic Line' running from Pesaro in the east to La Spezia in the west. With reserves being diverted to Southern England the stalemate of the Italian Campaign lasted until April 1945. The Allied spring offensive began on the 9th April. Bologna, Verona and Genoa soon fell to the Allied advance. Mussolini was captured by Italian Partisans in his attempt to escape to Switzerland. The 'Duce' (the leader) and his mistress were shot and strung up in a Milan garage. Fighting in the Italian Campaign was now at an end but for the troops that fought so long and hard, their achievements were overshadowed by the D-Day landings in Normandy.

DESCRIPTION: A six pointed star with the Royal monogram in the centre and the words 'THE ITALY STAR' below. Thr ribbon represents the Italian National colours-equal stripes of red, white, green, white and red.

METAL: Bronze

CLASPS: None issued

VALUATIONS: The Italy Star   £15 - £18

THE FRANCE & GERMANY STAR
6th June 1944 – 8th May 1945

The period of this award covers events from the D-Day Landings in Normandy on the 6th June 1944 to the final surrender of Germany on the 8th May 1945.

The area covered, despite its name, is all North West Europe including Belgium and The Netherlands. The British Channel Islands were 'bypassed' and the residents had to endure German occupation until the general surrender of German forces in the West. The Islands were liberated in May 1945 by 'Force 135'.

RAF, Royal and Merchant Naval personnel qualified for this medal by serving in the North Sea, English Channel and the Bay of Biscay. Gaining the 1939-45 Star was not a prerequisite for this medal.

The idea of an Allied invasion of Europe was first put into motion at the Washington Conference in May 1943. Codenamed 'Operation Overlord' it was initially planned for May 1944. The Southern Counties of England became a vast storehouse for war material and troops preparing for the greatest amphibious landing in history. Security was paramount.

German forces were now retreating in the East from the Russians and in the South from the Allies after Italy's collapse. Now was the time to open another front in North West Europe. It would be no easy ride for the Allies. The European coastline was heavily defended. Field Marshal Erwin Rommel (the Desert Fox) was now in command of the Atlantic Wall of Hitler's 'Fortress Europe'.

The Germans were aware that the invasion would come but they did not know where or when. Through devious means of false intelligence and the work of double agents the German High Command thought the main Allied invasion would come at the Pas de Calais – the shortest route across the Channel.

The Invasion was finally given the go ahead for the 6th June 1944 by the Supreme Commander of Allied forces General Eisenhower. The invasion would take place off the Cotentin Peninsula in Normandy.

In the early hours of the 6th June British Airborne troops, towed in gliders to the landing areas, were to secure bridges over the Caen Canal and the River Orne. Other British Airborne units would assault the German battery at Merville and then secure areas north of Ranville for further landings. Meanwhile the American Airborne Division secured objectives on the southeastern corner of the Cotentin Peninsula.

The beaches were codenamed 'Utah', 'Omaha', (American objectives), 'Gold', 'Juno' and 'Sword', (British and Canadian Objectives). Thirty minutes before the amphibious landings Royal Naval ships, under the command of Admiral Ramsey, bombarded German coastal defences, as the RAF and USAAF mounted a coordinated bombing offensive.

The British and Canadians on Gold, Juno and Sword faired reasonably well with less than expected casualties. The Americans on the other hand met hardened resistance and mistakes were made with their special amphibious tanks being launched too soon resulting in many troops being drowned before reaching the foreshore.

THE FRANCE & GERMANY STAR
6th June 1944 – 8th May 1945

Overall, Operation Overlord was a great success with 156,000 Allied troops ashore in Normandy on the first day. The feeling among many was that the worst of the fighting was over.

The battle for the Normandy beaches was now over – reserves were crossing the channel, supply lines were being prepared, temporary 'Mulberry' harbours were put in place, vast fuel pipelines were laid along the Channel seabed. There were however, hard battles still to be fought.

For the Americans their nemesis would be the Ardennes Offensive - 'The Battle of the Bulge', for the British it was 'Operation Market Garden' at Arnhem.

Montgomery's plan to shorten the war failed at Arnhem. The intention was to seize vital bridgeheads in Holland over the Rivers Maas, Waal and Lek and clear a path leading straight into the German heartland. It was a combined operation with American Airborne troops landing at Eindhoven and Nijmegen on 17th September 1944. Simultaneously British and Polish troops were dropped at Arnhem. Ground forces then linked up with the first two bridgeheads on the 18th & 19th September but because of mixed intelligence reports concerning German strength in the area they were unable to reach Arnhem. The British held out for 10 long days, 2,200 troops were evacuated; 7,000 were killed, wounded or taken prisoner.

The Ardennes offensive was over by the 26th December after the bad weather cleared and the Allies could regain air supremacy and slowly push on through Germany.

By the 21st March 1945 the Allies held a line from Holland to the Swiss border with a bridgehead over the Rhine at Remagen - the Ludendorff Bridge that had been taken intact by the American 1st Army just before it was to be blown up by the Germans. While US troops advanced towards Bavaria in Southern Germany Montgomery's troops made their way to Bremen (24th April), Lubeck (27th April), and Hamburg 2nd May.

The end of the war in Europe was now in sight. The Russian Armies were now fighting the last battles for Berlin. Fearing that he would end up hanging in humiliation as Mussolini had, Adolf Hitler committed suicide on 30th April 1945.

On the 7th May an unconditional surrender was signed. As the Second World War ended in Europe, another war - the Cold War - would begin, with an iron curtain splitting Europe into two armed camps for the next 50 years.

DESCRIPTION: A six pointed star with the Royal monogram in the centre and the words 'THE ATLANTIC STAR' below. The ribbon consists of equal stripes of red, white and blue representing the National colours of Britain, France and the Netherlands.

METAL: Bronze

CLASPS: ATLANTIC

VALUATIONS: The France & Germany Star   £20 - £25
with 'ATLANTIC' clasp add £60 - £70

THE FRANCE & GERMANY STAR
6th June 1944 – 8th May 1945

A small addressed box - Recipients, including Laurence McLaughlin of Northern Ireland (above) received their WWII medals in a small card box.

THE DEFENCE MEDAL

Awarded to British, Commonwealth forces and certain civilian organisations for three years' service between 1939-1945. It was also awarded to defenders, subject to air attack, in Malta, Gibraltar, Ceylon, Cyprus, West Africa and Palestine. The qualifying period for non-operational areas was one year. For areas threatened by air attacks the period was six months.

Civilian personnel included the Air Raid Wardens' Service (ARP), Fire Service, Ambulance Service, Police, Civil Defence and the Mortuary Service. It could be awarded singly or in addition to other campaign medals. The largest single group to receive this award was the Home Guard.

The Home Guard was, and still is, the butt of many jokes. The Home Guard were immortalised by the long running BBC comedy series 'Dads Army'. They played a vital part in the defence of the British Isles. In May 1940 the BEF, Belgian, Dutch and French troops were evacuated from the beaches of Dunkirk. 338,000 British and Allied troops would live to fight another day but vital equipment was left behind in the hasty withdrawal and the USA was still neutral. Britain was at its lowest ebb. The War Secretary, Anthony Eden, proposed a 'Local Defence Volunteer Force', later to become the Home Guard.

The Home Guard recruited men too young or too old to enlist in the regular Forces from the age group 17-65. As it was a 'part-time' organisation men in reserved occupations could also enlist. At first, equipment, arms and uniforms were in short supply but as the war progressed the Home Guard became well armed with British, American and Canadian manufactured armaments. Many of the older members of the Home Guard had already had military training as they had seen service in the Great War and/or Colonial conflicts. Their duties included guarding vital installations, coastal patrols, escorting enemy air crew to POW camps etc.

There were half a million men recruited into the Home Guard between May 1940 and December 1944 when they were officially dissolved. They were a well trained organisation giving reassurance to the general population when it was needed most and if there had been an enemy invasion the general consensus is that they would have fought just as well, if not better than the German equivalent of the Home Guard, the Volkssturm.

DESCRIPTION: Obverse - uncrowned head of George VI (similar to coinage of the period). Reverse - two Royal Lions with a crowned oak sapling in the centre signifying 'protection or defence'. The dates 1939 and 1945 are at the sides. Under the wavy lines of the sea are the words, 'THE DEFENCE MEDAL'.

RIBBON: Two broad stripes of green, representing Britain's green land, and narrow stripes of black (the Black-out), with a wide stripe of orange representing fire.

CLASPS: None issued

METAL: Cupro-Nickel, or Silver for the Canadian issue.

VALUATIONS: The Defence Medal £18 - £20

THE DEFENCE MEDAL

THE 1939 – 1945 WAR MEDAL

The War Medal was awarded to all British and Commonwealth service personnel who served a minimum period of 28 days, either in an operational or non-operational capacity between 3rd September 1939 to 2nd September 1945. It could be awarded singly or in addition to other campaign stars and the Defence Medal. Members of the Merchant Navy had to serve their 28 days at sea. The Home Guard was not eligible for this award.

DESCRIPTION: Obverse - the crowned head of King George VI. Reverse - British lion on top of a dragon signifying the defeat of the Axis powers. Above the lion is the date; 1939 1945.

RIBBON: A red stripe in the centre with white stripes on either side. Broad red stripes at the edges and two intervening stripes of blue, (the national colours).

CLASPS: None (but see Mentions in Despatches on the next page)

METAL: Cupro-Nickel, or Silver for the Canadian issue.

VALUATIONS: War Medal 1939-45 £12 - £15
Canadian Silver Version £18 - £20

The oak leaf attached to a recipients War Medal after a mention in despatches

MENTIONS IN DESPATCHES (M.I.D.)

An MID is an award for exceptional action in the field, written up in reports or despatches by a senior officer. The award itself could be said to be slightly less than a 'gallantry' award.

Awarded for action in the First World War it was represented by an oak leaf spray that could only be worn on the 1914-19 Victory Medal.

Second World War MIDs are a smaller oak leaf emblem worn only on the 1939-45 War Medal. In both examples only one MID can be shown.

The collector will often find MIDs in medal groups offered for sale. See image on previous page.

The Korean War 1950 – 1953

Background:

By the end of the Second World War most of the civilised world was split into two opposing beliefs and two armed camps. Communist-Russia, China, and the 'satellite' states, and the Capitalism of the USA and her Allies. Britain, once the greatest imperial power the world had ever known, was now reduced to the role of a 'junior partner' to the American economic giant.

Two World Wars and colonial commitments had bled Britain dry. From 1945 to the present day Great Britain would take a secondary position in the world to the USA.

After the devastating effects of the two atomic bombs dropped on Japan in August 1945 to force a Japanese surrender a race was now on for the Communists to develop their own atomic weapon. The Russian leader, Stalin, was quite happy to see other Communist states causing problems for the Americans and British. Luckily for the world, Korea was a 'conventional' war but the US had atomic bombs sent to Guam in preparation, in case of a Russian invasion of Japan.

The local situation in the Far East in 1949 was as follows; the Americans supported the Chinese Nationalists in Formosa (Taiwan). The Russians supported the Chinese Communists under the leadership of Mao-tse-Tung.

When the Japanese occupation of Korea ended in 1945 it was decided to draw up a 'demarcation' line between the Soviet backed North Korea and the Western, (mainly US and British backed), South Korea. The Demarcation line was the 38th parallel of latitude splitting the Korean peninsula virtually in half. There were attempts, mainly by British and American governments, to re-unite Korea under United Nations guidelines but Stalin blocked any progress.

The North Koreans, with Soviet military aid, intended to destabilize the South by guerrilla warfare before an all out invasion. With secret Russian support the North Koreans attacked with regular troops on 25th June 1950. US General MacArthur, Supreme Commander in the Far East went to Korea to investigate for himself. He recommended immediate military action to President Truman. Under UN Security Council resolutions US forces began to mobilise. Britain and other members of the Security Council supported the proposed American action.

THE KOREAN WAR 1950 – 1953 (continued)

US troops from the Army of Occupation in Japan were sent to Korea to aid the ailing South Korean Army. It soon became apparent that these undertrained troops were not prepared for combat and would not be able to hold their ground. After a 100 mile retreat and loss of equipment and heavy casualties a firm line was established on the River Naktong in the south of the country. Reinforcements were now arriving from the US.

The US was now looking for physical support from its Security Council Allies. Britain and the Commonwealth now acted. After Indian Independence (1947) there was a lack of manpower in the British forces. National Service filled some of the gaps and the term of service was increased from 18 months to 2 years. Britain was already fighting Communist insurgents in Malaya and Hong Kong had to be protected against a possible Chinese invasion.

In June 1950 a British Royal Naval squadron was sent to Korea. This was soon followed by the 29th Infantry Brigade and other troops from Hong Kong. Aircraft were sent from the Far East Fleet. By September detachments of Australian and New Zealand troops were sent to Korea.

The British and US were now striking back with air attacks on North Korean supply lines and communications. The North Korean forces now began a northerly retreat pushed back by US, British and Commonwealth troops. The question now was - would the UN Allies cross the 38th parallel?

General MacArthur approached the North Koreans for a cease-fire and disarmament. There was no response. In October the advance north continued. British and Australian units sped on to P'yongyang and the Ch'ongch'on taking many POWs on the way. Further reinforcements were now arriving from Britain.

MacArthur now wanted to land troops on the north east coast and force the North Koreans into surrender. Meanwhile Communist China was amassing 330,000 troops along its border with North Korea. At the end of October the Chinese began their night attacks. South Korean, US and British troops had to withdraw to re-group and organise their defences. By 25th December the British were in and around the Southern capital of Seoul.

On the 3rd January 1951 Chinese regular forces attacked British positions. The order was given to evacuate Seoul. Other Chinese troops, disguised as refugees, made the situation even worse. The British held the rearguard for the Americans. There was now panic in Washington and London but the UN forces slowly recovered over the next three months and there was a steady advance north again to the 38th parallel. The Communists were under constant air attacks. By April 1951 British and Commonwealth troops, including Canadians, were back in Seoul.

The Chinese were now regrouping with half a million troops being prepared for a major offensive. The main Chinese attack came on the 22nd April along the lower Imjin River. Most of the British 29th Brigade held the line. The Gloucesters became cut off and isolated. After many hours of close fighting some of the Regiment escaped, others were captured by the Chinese.

By the end of May the Chinese had retreated back above the 38th parallel. UN troops penetrated up to 20 miles beyond the line. It was now suggested by the Soviets to the UN in New York to draw up an armistice. Both sides met at Kaesong on 8th July 1951.

THE KOREA MEDAL 1950 – 1953
(Also referred to as 'the Queen's Korea Medal')

No agreement was reached until 1953 so the war continued into opposing entrenched lines with little movement. It was stalemate on the ground while the Royal Navy made its presence felt offshore destroying enemy shipping. UN air attacks increased in an attempt to break the deadlock.

After the death of Stalin in March 1953 the Chinese began to favour an end to hostilities mainly on financial grounds. In April 1953 it was agreed by the UN Security Council that there would be an exchange of POWs. This was the first step towards peace negotiations.

After further actions in May 1953 a ceasefire began on 27th July 1953. 66,000 British and Commonwealth troops served in Korea. The cost to the British economy was huge coming just five years' after the end of World War II. British forces served with distinction giving a much needed morale boost to their American Allies.

Issued for service in the Korean War between July 1950 and July 1953. Qualification for this award for land forces was one day's service in Korea. For the Royal Navy it was 28 days' operations off shore and for the RAF one or more operational sorties over the area. MIDs had to be worn on this medal ribbon.

DESCRIPTION: Obverse - Young bust of Elizabeth II (by Mary Gillick and also used on coinage until 1968). Reverse - Hercules wrestling the Hydra (Communism). The word 'KOREA' at the bottom.

RIBBON: Yellow with two blue stripes.

METAL: Cupro-Nickel, or Silver for the Canadian issue.

VALUATIONS:
Issued to the 'Glorious Gloucesters' £380 - £480
Other British Regiments £130 - £190
RAF/Royal Navy £200 - £675 Depending on
Regiment or Corps.
Commonwealth forces £125 - £160

THE UNITED NATIONS KOREA MEDAL

The UN Medal was awarded to all the international forces that took part in the Korean conflict, including all British and Commonwealth troops, between 1950-1953.

Qualification was one day's service in Korea or in support units in Japan. The qualifying period was later extended to July 1954 to include those who served in Korea after the armistice.

DESCRIPTION: Obverse - the wreathed emblem of the United Nations. Reverse - inscribed 'FOR SERVICE IN DEFENCE OF THE PRINCIPLES OF THE CHARTER OF THE UNITED NATIONS'.

RIBBON: UN colours of 17 alternating pale blue and white stripes.

METAL: Bronze

CLASP: The word 'KOREA' mounted on the ribbon that is part of the suspension of the medal.

VALUATION: £25 - £30

THE GENERAL SERVICE MEDAL 1962
(Also referred to as the 'Campaign Services Medal')

Awarded to all branches of the Armed Forces. Instituted in 1964 for minor campaigns from 1962-1999. There are 13 campaign clasps. The most common being 'NORTHERN IRELAND' with 130,000 issued. The rarest clasp is 'SOUTH VIETNAM' with only 70 awarded.

The 13 clasps are as follows:

1. BORNEO

Awarded for action in Borneo and Brunei between 1962-1966. At the end of WWII North Borneo and Sarawak became Crown Colonies. Brunei remained a Protectorate.

The first insurrection from Indonesian backed rebels from Brunei came in December 1962 when they attacked Shell oil workers in Seria. This incursion was soon put down. A greater incursion came in April 1963 when Indonesian troops crossed the border from Kalimantan and killed police personnel at Tebeda. Further confrontation continued for nearly four years along the 900-mile border between North Borneo and Kalimantan before the Indonesians were brought to the conference table. Much of the action along the border had been covert with SAS and Gurkha raids across the border into Kalimantan (operation Claret).

All British and Commonwealth troops were under the command of General Walker who was a great believer in inter-service co-operation in the field between ground troops, RAF and the Navy. Lessons had been learnt after the fall of Malaya and Singapore to the Japanese in 1941 and from the 12 year long Malayan Emergency (1948-1960). Ironically some Indonesian officers and NCO's had been trained at the British Jungle Warfare School in Malaya. British casualties consisted of 114 fatal and 200 wounded; Indonesian losses were estimated at 600 killed and 700 captured.

2. RADFAN (Apr -July 1964) & 3. SOUTH ARABIA (Aug 1964 - Nov 1967)

The Radfan was a small tribal region between Yemen to the north and the British protectorate of Aden in the south of Arabia. Radfan tribes, encouraged by the Egyptian backed National Liberation Front from Yemen, began anti-British terrorist attacks in December 1963 with the attempted assassination of the British High Commissioner. Reinforcements were first sent from Britain and Kenya for what would be Britain's last 'colonial' war. With air support and the timely arrival of the SAS and Royal Marine Commando units the Radfan was made secure before all British troops withdrew to Aden and the region was left in the hands of the newly formed South Arabian Army.

In 1966 the British Labour Government decided that all British Forces would leave Aden by 1968. Bitter rivalry and fighting now began between the National Liberation Front (N.L.F.) and the Front for the Liberation of South Yemen (F.L.O.S.S.Y.), with the British caught in the middle of these factions. There was a well-planned and executed evacuation of all British troops and civilians from the area. British troops were on full alert as the hand over ceremony was performed and the Union Jack was lowered. While the NLF and FLOSSY fought between themselves a Royal Naval task force arrived with 24 ships, to cover the last withdrawing units. By the end of November the British Governor and the last few Royal Marines left Aden to the NLF, ending a British presence in South Arabia that had lasted for 128 years.

THE GENERAL SERVICE MEDAL 1962 (continued)

The 13 clasps, continued:

4. MALAY PENINSULA (Aug 1964 - Aug 1966)

The campaign for this clasp is related to actions already mentioned on the previous page for BORNEO when Indonesian troops rebelled in Malaya against British and local forces.

5. SOUTH VIETNAM (Dec 1962 - May 1964)

This clasp was only awarded to Australian personnel working with forces of the Republic of South Vietnam.

6. NOTHERN IRELAND (August 1969 onwards)

Awarded for 30 or more days' peacekeeping operations in the troubled Northern Ireland region.

7. DHOFAR (Oct 1969 - Sep 1976)

Dhofar is situated between South Yemen and Oman. As with Aden the main British interest in the region had been the protection of its trade routes to Imperial India. In 1915 and 1957 military aid had been given to put down local insurgents. A formal agreement had been reached in 1958 whereby Britain would send officers to train the newly formed Sultan's Armed Forces (S.A.F.).

After Britain withdrew from Aden the Communists, mainly Soviet, sought to control Oman by Russian backed Dhofari and Yemeni dissidents. In 1970 a new Sultan came to power in a bloodless coup. Money soon became available for civil institutions and the build-up and modernisation of the SAF. The Sultan called for an amnesty for the communist rebels in the Jebel region. Two squadrons of the SAS began a 'hearts and minds' operation in the Jebel gaining much support from the Dhofari tribesmen.

In 1971 a permanent base was established in the central Jebel (Operation Jaguar). From this base enemy supply lines could be harassed. Another base was established at Sarfait close to the South Yemen border. In July 1972 a small team of SAS troops supported the newly formed Firqa soldiers (ex-rebels), in an action at Marbat.

Outnumbered by the rebels, support was called up from the Sultan of Oman's Air Force. The rebels lost political standing by the loss of this battle. During 1973 defensive lines were drawn up along the 30 mile long Hornbeam Line by British Engineer Squadrons on loan with cover provided by Jordanian troops sent in support by King Hussein. By December 1973 the writing was on the wall for communist rebels. More aid, in the form of troops and helicopters, came from the Shah of Iran. With Iranian, and crack units from Jordan, the conflict was all but over by 1975 with only 'mopping-up' operations to end the rebellion.

8. LEBANON (Feb 1983- March 1984)

Only 700 clasps awarded to British personnel as part of the Multinational Peacekeeping Force after the Israeli invasion of The Lebanon.

THE GENERAL SERVICE MEDAL 1962 (continued)

The 13 clasps, continued:

9. MINE CLEARANCE (Aug - Oct 1984)

Awarded to Royal Naval personnel engaged in mine clearance operations in the Gulf of Suez

10. GULF (November 1986 - February 1989)

Awarded mainly to Royal Naval personnel engaged in patrol and intelligence operations during the Iran/Iraq War.

11. KUWAIT (March - Sep 1991)

Awarded for service in Kuwait after the Gulf War of 1990.

12. N. IRAQ & S. TURKEY

Awarded mainly to RAF personnel enforcing the 'no fly zone' over Kurdish territory after the 1990 Gulf War

13. AIR OPERATIONS IRAQ

Awarded mainly to RAF personnel engaged in air patrols over Iraq after the first early 1990's Gulf War.

DESCRIPTION: Obverse - crowned bust of Elizabeth II. Reverse - Crown above the words, FOR CAMPAIGN SERVICE, surrounded by an oak wreath. The clasp(s) are mounted above a curved ornate suspension.

RIBBON: Purple with green at the edges.

METAL: Silver

VALUATIONS:

BORNEO	£75 - £95
RADFAN	£95 - £130
SOUTH ARABIA	£60 - £110
MALAY PENINSULA	£75 - £100
NORTHERN IRELAND	£60 - £90
DHOFAR	£160 - £205
LEBANON	£710 - £820
MINE CLEARANCE	£820 - £1030
GULF	£250 - £290
KUWAIT	£410 - £460
N. IRAQ & S. TURKEY	£360 - £460
AIR OPERATIONS IRAQ	£365 - £465

THE GENERAL SERVICE MEDAL 1962 (continued)

ACCUMULATED CAMPAIGN SERVICE MEDAL

Instituted in 1994 this is technically a 'long service' award but is related to the General Service Medal (1962), covered on the previous pages. The Accumulated Campaign Service Medal can be awarded to all service personnel who already have the General Service Medal (1962) and then go on to accumulate further periods of 36 months campaign service since August 1969. Service with the UN and NATO does not count towards this award.

DESCRIPTION: Obverse - crowned head of Elizabeth II. Reverse - The inscription from top to bottom, 'FOR ACCUMULATED CAMPAIGN SERVICE' set in a ribbon surrounded by oak and laurel leaves around the inscription.

RIBBON: Purple and green with a central gold stripe.

METAL: Hallmarked silver.

CLASPS: Awarded for each period of service (36 months).

VALUATION: £250 - £350

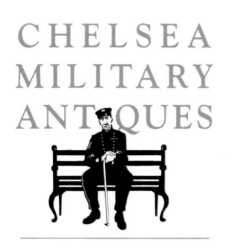

RHODESIA MEDAL 1980

This medal was awarded to British and Commonwealth forces who took part in the security arrangements relating to the free elections held before independence between 1st December 1979 and 20th March 1980. After independence was granted Rhodesia became the Republic of Zimbabwe.

Northern Rhodesia, (now Zambia, independent since 1964), and Southern Rhodesia were named after the great Imperial expansionist, Cecil Rhodes. The country was discovered by the explorer David Livingstone but it was Cecil Rhodes who wanted to extend the British Empire from the Cape through Central Africa all the way to Cairo.

Already the head of the British South Africa Company, Rhodes obtained mineral rights in the area occupied by the Matabele and then peacefully occupied what was to be called Southern Rhodesia in 1890 and founded the capital, Salisbury, (after the British Prime minister, Lord Salisbury).

Rhodes' dream of a railway from the Cape to Cairo was never fulfilled but the project reached Bulawayo in 1897 and the Victoria Falls in 1903. Rhodes' South African Company administered Southern Rhodesia until 1923 when the country became internally self-governing under British Empire rule.

As much as the British Government tried to safeguard the rights of the Black community in Southern Rhodesia the 1930 Land Apportionment Act gave the white Europeans half the land area, including all mining and industrial interests.

In 1953 a federation was formed between Nyasaland, Northern and Southern Rhodesia. Southern Rhodesia dominated the federation and it was feared by the native populations that a South African style of 'apartheid' might be introduced by the largely right-wing government.

Lord Malvern, (a former Southern Rhodesian PM and first PM of the Federation), wanted the federation to have Dominion Status within the British Commonwealth. The Black majority feared they would lose what little protection they had from Britain if this action arose. The Federation came to an end when Nyasaland and Northern Rhodesia withdrew in 1963.

Through the 1960's and 70's Rhodesia was a thorn in Britain's side. Whilst Britain was trying to bow out gracefully from the concept of Empire, the Commonwealth at large was not happy with the white minority rule in Rhodesia. Newly independent African countries were pressing Britain for an independent Rhodesia.

On the 11th November 1965 Premier Ian Smith of Rhodesia declared UDI (Unilateral Declaration of Independence) without British consent therefore maintaining white supremacy. Harold Wilson's Labour government in London imposed 'economic' sanctions on Rhodesia and negotiations between London and Salisbury continued to no avail.

RHODESIA MEDAL 1980

Under pressure from all sides Ian Smith finally agreed in 1976 to majority rule within a two year timeframe. An Internal Settlement was then reached with the African Nationalists. The Patriotic Front parties, led by Robert Mugabe opted for guerrilla warfare against the Government of Rhodesia.

In 1979 Britain agreed to establish an independent Rhodesia, (to be known as Zimbabwe) and the Patriotic Front parties would be allowed to participate in free elections. The joint British and Rhodesian force (including British Police officers) would oversee the ceasefire and elections.

The Patriotic Front parties under Robert Mugabe won the elections for an independent Zimbabwe and Commonwealth membership. Whether black Africans under Mugabe's rule are now any happier is a matter for conjecture.

DESCRIPTION: Obverse - crowned head of Elizabeth II, type as used for South Atlantic medal on the next pages. Reverse - a sable antelope with the words, THE RHODESIA MEDAL, and the date 1980.

RIBBON: Light blue, a narrow strip of red, white and dark blue in the centre.

METAL: cupro-nickel.

VALUATION: £375-£475

Note: The medal was awarded named to the armed forces, but not to Police personnel.

THE SOUTH ATLANTIC MEDAL

For service in the Falkland Islands' War, April – July 1982. Qualification for this highly prized award was at least one day's service in the Falklands or South Georgia or 30 days in the campaign zone including Ascension Island, (a British supply base in the mid-Atlantic).

The campaign was fought to liberate the Falkland Islands from the Argentine invasion. The Falkland Islands are situated in the South Atlantic 400 miles off the coast of Argentina. This small group of islands had been under British rule since 1832 and became a Crown Colony in 1962. The islands had been claimed by Argentina for over a hundred years. To divert attention from internal political problems in Argentina, President Galtieri and the ruling Junta decided in April 1982 to invade the quiet Falkland Islands.

In March 1982 Argentine 'scrap metal' workers and marines landed on South Georgia Island. This incident was followed, on 2nd April, by an amphibious landing by Argentine marines at Port Stanley the island's capital on East Falkland. Outnumbered, the Governor, Rex Hunt, gave the order to surrender to the small detachment of 70 Royal Marines.

As a result of intelligence reports received in the UK, a task force was made ready by the end of April for despatch to the South Atlantic. The force was led by the carriers Invincible and Hermes. South Georgia Island was retaken on 25th April by commando units, SBS and SAS troops. By May 1st the task force had arrived off the islands. The first job in the total exclusion zone was to harass the enemy and prepare for amphibious landings. Briefings had already begun on the journey from the UK. The Argentine battleship Belgrano was sunk on the 2nd May. This action totally demoralised the Argentine navy.

To enable the retaking of the main islands of East and West Falkland to be successful it was essential for the British task force to gain control of the skies. The most formidable part of the Argentine Armed Forces was the 'Fuerza Aerea', the Air Force. On May 1st a Vulcan bomber dropped twenty-one 1000lb bombs on to the Argentine held airfield at Port Stanley. The Vulcan had flown from Ascension Island and had been refuelled en route in mid air on the 12 hour flight. The resulting damage meant that the Argentines could no longer take off from the Islands.

The star of the air war was the Hawker Harrier. In 1980 the Naval version, the Sea Harrier replaced the faster jets on aircraft carriers. At the start of hostilities there were only twenty Sea Harriers in the task force - twelve on Invincible and eight on Hermes - against some two hundred Argentine aircraft including Mirages and Skyhawks. With echoes of the 1940 Battle of Britain the Argentine pilots had little time to spend over the Islands as they had been instructed to avoid confrontation with the Harriers and concentrate on attacks on British ships.

The Harriers, the 'few' in this case, were kept in the air as much as possible. Unfortunately two Harriers were lost in a bad weather collision on the second day. Even with the tragic loss of the cargo ship 'Atlantic Conveyor', on May 26th 6 RAF Harriers were brought into the theatre to aid in the protection of ground forces on the attack of Port Stanley and Goose Green.

THE SOUTH ATLANTIC MEDAL

The Argentines surrendered on the 14th June. Twenty-nine Argentinean aircraft had been shot down and nine had been destroyed on the ground. There had been no Harriers lost to enemy action.

A total of 29,682 of these medals were awarded. Servicemen and Women in the Royal Navy received the most with a total of 12,927 awarded.

DESCRIPTION: Obverse - Crowned head of Elizabeth II. Reverse - Falkland Island Arms surrounded by the words 'SOUTH ATLANTIC MEDAL' and a laurel wreath below the arms.

RIBBON: Watered silk, blue, white, green, white and blue.

METAL: Cupro-nickel.

CLASPS: Rosette on the ribbon to denote service in the combat zone.

VALUATIONS:

Without combat zone rosette   £220 - £300

Army (7000 issued)	£420 - £520 with combat zone rosette
Royal Navy (13000 issued)	£360 - £460 with combat zone rosette
Royal Marines (3700 issued)	£620 - £930 with combat zone rosette
RAF (2000 issued)	£360 - £420 with combat zone rosette
Fleet Aux. (2000 issued)	£360 - £460 with combat zone rosette
Parachute regiment	£820 - £1230 with combat zone rosette
Merchant Navy	£360 - £410 with combat zone rosette

The last of the Fleet Air Arm's Sea Harrier squadron was disbanded in March 2006.

South Atlantic medal with combat zone rosette.

THE GULF WAR MEDAL 1990 - 91

Awarded for 30 days' continuous service in the Middle East, including Cyprus, between 2nd August 1990 and 7th March 1991 during the liberation of Kuwait - codenamed 'Desert Storm'.

By 1989 Iraq, under the dictator Saddam Hussein, had become the most powerful country in the Gulf region. During the Iran/Iraq War Saddam had built up a powerful army of over half a million men, 4000 tanks and 700 combat aircraft. There was also an added danger of the possible use of chemical or biological weapons by the Iraqi dictator.

The claim by Iraq on the oil rich state of Kuwait went back many years. On the 2nd August 1990 Iraqi forces crossed the Iraq/Kuwait border soon eliminating the small Kuwait forces to take control of the country

The first part of the campaign was the build-up of Coalition forces in response to the UN ultimatum to Iraq to withdraw their troops from Kuwait by 15th January 1991. The main members of the Coalition were the US, Britain, France and Saudi Arabia. Tactical headquarters for the Coalition was based in Riyadh in Saudi Arabia. Aircraft from Britain were based at five main airfields in and around Saudi Arabia and the Gulf. The Royal Navy maintained its presence, as it had throughout the Iran/Iraq War, in the Gulf. The Navy had great effect in mine clearance and maintaining the blockade against Iraq. In the meantime the 1st British Division were preparing for deployment into Southern Iraq.

The first attack on Iraq began in the early hours of 17th January by 2000 Coalition aircraft including RAF Tornados and Jaguars. RAF Tornados were employed in bombing Iraqi airfields using the 'JP233' weapons system rendering enemy airfields inoperable.

There was virtually no response from the Iraqi Airforce except a large number of pilots, with their aircraft, defected to Iran. However, there was a very real danger from enemy anti-aircraft ground fire and one Tornado was lost on the 18th January. After a further loss of another two Tornados (the crews were taken prisoner), it was decided to change from low level night attacks with JP233, to day attacks using conventional bombs at medium level.

After the Coalition had gained air superiority the political pressure was on to counter the threat to Israel from Iraqi Scud missiles. Six specially equipped RAF Tornados were used to detect the mobile Scud launchers. Specialist ground forces were also engaged in the search but less successfully.

Because of mounting civilian casualties in Baghdad and other areas, RAF Buccaneer aircraft were sent out to the Gulf on January 23rd to 'mark' targets for the Tornado crews. An even greater degree of precision was achieved.

The ground attack began on 24th February. Iraqi forces, by this time, had been worn down by constant air attacks during the weeks leading up to the advance across the Saudi Arabian border with Kuwait. Enemy supply and communication lines were now in chaos. Even the defences of Saddam's elite 'Republican Guard' were in disarray.

THE GULF WAR MEDAL 1990-91

By the 26th February Coalition forces were advancing on to Kuwait City. Demoralized and panic-stricken Iraqi troops began to retreat back along the main road north to Basra in Iraq. Two days later on 28th February Iraqi commanders signed an unconditional surrender.

The first Gulf War was now over, resulting in the loss of 44 Coalition troops. Over 80,000 Iraqi POW's were taken and many casualties inflicted on Saddam's troops.

DESCRIPTION: Obverse - crowned head of Elizabeth II.
Reverse - an eagle (RAF), automatic rifle (Army) and an anchor (Royal Navy)
The words 'THE GULF WAR' and the dates, 1990-91.

RIBBON: Colours representing the desert and the three Services.

METAL: Cupro-nickel.

CLASPS: '2 AUG 1990' and '16 JAN TO 28 FEB 1991'.

VALUATIONS:

Gulf Medal (without clasp)	£160-£190
With clasp '2 AUG 1990'	£2000-£3000
'16 JAN TO 28 FEB 1991'	£220-£360

UNITED NATIONS MEDALS

Of the 40 UN Medals issued to date the most significant for British forces are KOREA 1951 - 53 as shown on page 60, CYPRUS 1964 to date and for service in Bosnia UNPROFOR 1992 - 95 shown on page 75.

UN CYPRUS MEDAL - 1964 TO DATE

The beautiful island of Cyprus in the Mediterranean has a long and fascinating history, from Stone-age settlements to colonization by the ancient Greeks and Phoenicians. In more recent times Cyprus became a British Crown Colony in 1925.

For centuries the Greek and Turkish Cypriots lived separate lives in suspicion of each other. The Greek population outnumbered the Turkish by 4-1. Divisions were based on culture and religion. The island was an important military and naval base for Britain being situated near Egypt and the Suez Canal - the lifeline to Britain's Indian Empire.

From 1955 the Greek majority wanted independence from Britain and union with mainland Greece. The result was the formation of the Greek - Cypriot guerrilla organisation called EOKA - Ethniki Organosis Kyprion Agoniston. In English the name translates to: The National Organisation of Cypriot Fighters. The group was led by George Grivas. A reign of terror was unleashed on Turkish Cypriots, British Servicemen and any Greek Cypriots they considered to be traitors to their cause.

Turkish and Greek relations within NATO became very strained. The head of the Orthodox Church, Archbishop Makarios, was deported by the British for his implication in the terrorist campaign.

With a danger of an all-out Greek/Turkish War, agreement was reached at talks in London and Zurich. Cyprus became a republic in 1960 with a Greek Cypriot president (Makarios), and a Turkish Cypriot vice president. Britain kept her bases near Limassol and Cyprus joined the Commonwealth in 1961.

The troubles were not yet over, Problems continued between the two populations on the island. In 1974 there was a Greek backed coup and Makarios was deposed. 1976 saw the Turkish invasion of the island led by air-borne troops resulting in a partition of the island. The UN would hold the line between the two opposing sides with its peacekeeping operation, which still continues to this day.

At the height of the terror campaign in the late 1950's, 156 British Servicemen lost their lives.

DESCRIPTION: Obverse - Globe surrounded by wreath with 'UN' above. Reverse - The inscription 'IN THE SERVICE OF PEACE'.

RIBBONS: White centre bordered to the left and right with a thin stripe of dark blue and a broaded stripe of pale blue.

METAL: Bronze

CLASPS: None

VALUATIONS: Cyprus UN Medal £25 - £35 (Original Striking)

UN CYPRUS MEDAL - 1964 TO DATE

UN BOSNIA UNPROFOR MEDAL
(United Nations Protection Force)

The historically troubled area of the Balkans is where British troops attached to the UN Peacekeeping force were sent in 1992.

The population of the region is divided by different ethnic, religious and political groups. During, and after World War II the Yugoslav leader, Tito, with Soviet support, had managed to keep order between the Croats, Serbs and Slovenes.

Marshal Tito became president in 1953. By the time of his death in 1980 Yugoslavia was beginning to break up. In 1989 the late Slobodan Milosevic became president of Serbia with the backing of the Yugoslav Federal Army. In 1991 Slovenia and Croatia declared independence. Fighting broke out between the Yugoslav Federal Army (JNA) and Slovene Defence Forces.

After many civilian deaths and atrocities committed in Vukovar a cease-fire was signed in January 1992 and the UNPROFOR was sent into the area to do the difficult job of keeping the opposing factions apart.

The three opposing sides in Bosnia were the Bosnian Muslims, the Serbs and the Croats. The UN mandate was that troops in the Protection Force could only retaliate in 'self defence'. With the risk of sniper fire British troops protected relief convoys and helped support the growing number of refugees.

In February 1994 the Markele market in Sarajevo was the scene of slaughter when a mortar bomb killed 68 people and injured many more. Lieutenant General Sir Michael Rose, at that time UNPROFOR commander in Bosnia, decided enough was enough and threatened the opposing Serbs and Muslims with NATO air strikes. The end result was a cease-fire and the Cessation of Hostilities Agreement was signed in December. The hardest part of the Agreement for the UN peacekeepers was maintaining the security of the six 'safe areas'.

On the 15th April 1994 Corporal Rennie of the Parachute Regiment was killed when investigating cease-fire violations around Gorazde. General Rose called air strikes by Sea Harriers from the Royal Navy. Unfortunately one aircraft was destroyed by a shoulder-launched rocket - the pilot ejected from the plane and survived.

On April 29th a British patrol came under fire from Serb positions. Three Serbs were killed and the remainder were driven off. In the summer of 1995 all six of the safe areas came under attack from Serbs.

The new British commander, General Smith, called for air strikes when the Serbs seized weapons from the UN Collection sites. The Serbs retaliated by taking 400 UN hostages, including 28 Welsh Fusiliers who were eventually released after negotiations with President Milosevic. In August there was a major offensive by the Croats in the Krajina area making 150,000 Serbs homeless.

Pressure was now on from the American and European governments to put an end to the war after the murder of civilians who were loaded on to 70 buses and driven away to be massacred after the Serb attack on Srebrenica.

On the 28th August there was another attack on the Markele market area in Sarajevo killing 37 civilians. General Smith ordered NATO air attacks on Serb positions.

UN BOSNIA UNPROFOR MEDAL
(United Nations Protection Force)

On the 14ᵗʰ September a cease-fire was agreed and a peace settlement negotiated at Dayton, Ohio in the US and was finally signed in Paris in December.

The British troops in UNPROFOR now became part of the NATO Implementation Force. Besides helping local communities in the war torn region they also assisted in hunting down war criminals and bringing them to justice.

DESCRIPTION: As the UN Cyprus Medal on previous pages.

RIBBONS: Different designs usually incorporating the UN colours, blue and white.

METAL: Bronze

CLASPS: None on UNPROFOR. The later UNCRO (UN Confidence Restoration in Croatia 1995 - 96) was issued with a 'UNCRO' clasp.

VALUATIONS: All UN Medals (except Korea and Cyprus) £15 - £25

NATO SERVICE MEDALS 'KOSOVO' & 'FORMER YUGOSLAVIA'
Instituted December 1994

Awarded to British and NATO troops for 30 days' service in the former Yugoslavia or 60 days' related service outside the region.

The region of Kosovo is surrounded by its larger neighbours of Serbia to the north and east, Montenegro to the west, with Albania and Macedonia to the south. Under Marshal Tito of Yugoslavia, Kosovo had self-government. This arrangment was withdrawn in 1989 by President Slobodan Milosevic of Serbia. There was also internal tension between the two ethnic groups – the Kosovar Albanians and the Kosovar Serbs.

The Kosovar Albanian population in 1998 numbered 2 million, to 200,000 Kosovar Serbs. The Serbs controlled the Police and Army units and the Kosovar Albanians had their own unofficial president. In 1995 the Albanian backed Kosovar Liberation Army (KLA) began attacks on Serb police and security units. There then followed retaliatory attacks by Serb police units. The fighting soon spread across the country with the massacre of civilians and reports of atrocities relating to both sides.

In January 1999 the Serb government in Belgrade was given an ultimatum by Western Governments to withdraw their support for the Serbs in Kosovo or face NATO bombing and air strikes. The Serbs rejected demands from the West and NATO commenced air strikes on Belgrade on 24th March 1999. RAF Harriers attacked from NATO bases in Italy and the submarine, HMS Splendid, launched Tomahawk missiles from the Adriatic.

After 78 days of air attacks the Belgrade government agreed to withdraw their forces. On 12th June NATO forces, including five British battalions, entered Kosovo under the UN Security Council Resolution 1244.

In 2000 all three branches of the British Armed forces were still involved in peacekeeping and support duties in Bosnia and Kosovo. UN troops are still stationed in the region for peacekeeping purposes.

DESCRIPTION: Obverse - the NATO Star surrounded by a wreath. Reverse - the wording; 'IN SERVICE OF PEACE AND FREEDOM' in English and French with 'NORTH ATLANTIC TREATY ORGANISATION' in English and French around the outer rim.

RIBBON: The UN Colours of blue and white in various formations. 8 types in total.

METAL: Bronze

CLASPS: 'KOSOVO' and 'FORMER YUGOSLAVIA'

VALUATIONS: Both UN Medals £18- £20

NATO SERVICE MEDALS 'KOSOVO' & 'FORMER YUGOSLAVIA'
Instituted December 1994

THE OPERATIONAL SERVICE MEDAL (2000)

The new Operational Service Medal introduced in 1999 and effective from January 1st 2000, now replaces the General Service Medal (1962) except for service in Northern Ireland and Air Operations over Iraq war, which are still covered by the General Service Medal 1962. This new medal is awarded to all UK armed forces (subject to minimum qualification times) for campaigns for which there is no UN or NATO medal.

Ever since the great days of Empire, Afghanistan has been problematic for Britain. In the 19th Century the country acted as a buffer state between Imperial Russia and British Imperial India. In more recent times the mountainous region has been the hiding place of the Islamic dissident Osama Bin Laden and other members of his al-Qaeda group. Since the events in New York on September 11th 2001 and other subsequent terrorist attacks, British troops have been part of a coalition force with the US, (total 19,000 at present), to hunt down and capture the ever evasive Bin Laden and his followers. There is also a force of 9,000 NATO peace-keeping troops based mainly in the capital Kabul.

The former British colony of Sierra Leone had suffered many years of tribal fighting with tens of thousands of men (and young boys) under arms. Since 2002 Britain has led an international force to disarm the rebels and militia after approximately 50,000 deaths in the country.

DESCRIPTION: Obverse - Crowned bust of Queen Elizabeth II. Reverse - Eight compass points with Union flag in the centre and the words 'FOR OPERATIONAL SERVICE'. Each of the four corners of the compass arrows contains a crown.

RIBBON: The first type, for Sierra Leone has a thick red centre stripe flanked on either side by stripes of pale blue and then dark blue, with green edges. The Afganistan medal has sand coloured edges instead of green.

METAL: Cupro-nickel

CLASPS: 'AFGANISTAN' and 'SIERRA LEONE'.

VALUATIONS: £450 - £550

THE IRAQ MEDAL (2004)
(Operation TELIC)

The Iraq medal is awarded for service and support of operations in Iraq and elsewhere in the Gulf region from January 20th 2003 to the time of writing. It can be awarded to British armed forces, civilian personnel, embedded media, and also certain foreign nationals. Personnel who served in Iraq or Kuwait for seven continuous days between 19th March to the 28th April 2003 qualify for a clasp with those dates inscribed on it. Aircrew based outside of Iraq who flew two or more times into Iraq/Kuwait between the dates on the clasp also qualify for the clasp.

DESCRIPTION: Obverse - Crowned bust of Queen Elizabeth II. Reverse - Mythical Assyrian Sphinx (or Lamassu).

RIBBON: Thin white stripe in the centre with thin red stripe to the right (from the perspective of the onlooker) and a thin white stripe to the left. The edges are thick yellow/sand colour.

METAL: Cupro-nickel.

CLASPS: '19 MAR TO 28 APR 2003'

VALUATIONS: None Available

MINIATURE MEDALS & RIBBONS

In recent years there has been an increasing interest in collecting Miniature medals and Medal ribbons.

The quality of miniatures often varies according to which jeweller has produced the half-size replicas of the originals. Because of their convenient size, they are usually worn on formal occasions, such as regimental dinners etc.

Miniature medals always look more impressive in groups rather than singly and are a lot cheaper to buy than the full size versions. Some collectors will be offered groups of miniatures with the original full size versions. Always look for proof of authenticity.

Medal ribbon groups can also be purchased by the collector at reasonable prices. The collector will soon recognise which medals the ribbons were designed for.

Some examples are below and on the next page:

Miniatures
1. Boer War & WWI group.
2. World War II group (including an OBE on the left)
3. World War II group with QEII Coronation & Territorial medals
4. World War II group
5. GSM 1962 (Northern Ireland & UN Medal for Cyprus)
6. Military Medal (QEII) & Gulf Medal 1991

1.

2.

MINIATURE MEDALS & RIBBONS

3.

4.

5.

6.

MINIATURE MEDALS & RIBBONS (continued)

SINGLE BRITISH MINIATURE MEDAL VALUATIONS:

Queen's South Africa Medal	£20 - £50
King's South Africa Medal	£15 - £25
Queen's Mediterranean Medal	£60 - £70
Transport Medal 1903	£60 - £120
China War Medal 1900	£25 - £65
Ashanti Medal 1901	£30 - £60
Tibet Medal 1903 (The higher prices include the clasp)	£35 - £65
Africa General Service Medal 1902 - 1956	£35 - £80
India General Service Medal 1908 - 1935	£20 - £40
Khedive's Sudan Medal 1910	£60 - £80
1914 Star	£5 - £10
1914 - 15 Star	£5 - £8
British War Medal 1914 - 1918 (Bronze)	£6 - £25
WWI Victory Medal	£5 - £25
WWI Victory Medal Awarded to South African Serviceman	£75 - £85
Mercantile Marine War Medal	£25 - £30
Territorial Force War Medal	£25 - £30
Naval General Service Medal 1915 - 1962	£20 - £70
General Service Medal 1918 - 1962	£20 - £65
India General Service Medal 1936 - 1939	£15 - £35
1939 - 1945 Star	£5 - £10
Atlantic Star	£5 - £10
Air Crew Europe Star	£8 - £12
Africa Star	£5 - £15
Pacific Star	£5 - £10
Burma Star	£5 - £10
Italy Star	£5
France and Germany Star	£5 - £10
Defence Medal	£10 - £15
1939 - 1945 War Medal	£10 - £15
1939 - 1945 War Medal with Oak Leaf MID	£15 - £20
Korea Medal (Queen's Korea Medal)	£15 - £18
UN Korea Medal	£5 - £10
General Service Medal 1962	£10 - £25
Accumulated Campaign Service Medal	None Available
Rhodesia Medal 1980	
South Atlantic Medal 1982	£15 - £20
Gulf War Medal 1990 - 91	£15 - £20
Cyprus UN Medal 1964 onwards	£8 - £10
Bosnia UN Medal 1992 - 1995	£8 - £10
Kosovo NATO Medal	£10 - £12
Former Yugoslavia NATO Medal	£10 - £12
Operational Service Medal (2000)	None Available
Iraq Medal (2003 - date)	None Available

IRISH REPUBLIC (ÉIRE) MEDAL AWARDS

In December 1921 Ireland, excluding the six counties of Ulster, became the Irish Free State with dominion status within the British Empire. In 1949 the Irish Free State withdrew from the Commonwealth, changed its name to Éire and became a republic.

Catholic and Protestant Irishmen have always served with distinction in the British armed forces. During WWI, due to political tensions, conscription was not introduced in Ireland. Nevertheless, 140,000 Irishmen joined the British forces, of which 65,000 were Catholic. 20,000 Irishmen volunteered during the troubled times between 1919 and 1921. During WWII the Irish Defence Forces were greatly expanded.

Irish Republican Medal awards cover the period from 1916 to the present day, with Irish troops serving abroad as part of UN contingents. For example, in 1960 two battalions of Irish troops served in the Congo. This was the first time in the Republic's history that Irish soldiers had served outside Éire. Some of these troops were awarded the highest Irish Gallantry award, the Military Medal for Gallantry (AN BONN MILEATA CALMACHTA)

Other Irish UN commitments have included the Observation Group in Lebanon 1958, the United Nations Force in Cyprus from 1964 onwards, the United Nations Interim Force in Lebanon 1980 and the United Nations Mission in Kosovo from 1999 to date.

To date there have been 82 fatalities in the Irish Defence Forces whilst serving under the United Nations flag.

The prices given for Irish medals are in British Pounds Sterling, and it is worth noting that due to the rarity of some of these medals and therefore the lack of medals for sale on which to base price data, some of the medals do have quite wide price ranges. Lastly, appologies to Gaelic speakers, as the typesetter was not able to reproduce some of the interesting accents on Gaelic letters!

THE IRISH 1916 MEDAL

Instituted by the Irish Government in 1942 to commemorate the Easter Uprising in Dublin, April 1916. This award takes precedence over all other Irish medals.

The British Government's Third Home Rule Bill, after the House of Lords had tried in vain to veto the Bill, became law in May 1914. Under the terms of the Bill, the protestants of Ulster objected to being ruled by a predominately Catholic parliament in Dublin. The Ulstermen prepared to resist by force and raised 100,000 men, known as the 'Ulster Volunteers'. In March 1914 British Army officers from the Carragh Camp, sympathetic to the Ulster cause, resigned their commissions. Doubts were raised as to whether the British Army in Ulster would be able to implement the Home Rule Bill, and civil war loomed on the horizon.

In retaliation a force of 'National Volunteers' was raised in the South. King George V, seeing imminent dangers of the situation called the opposing parties to a conference in London in June 1914. Unfortunately the talks had little effect. Events in Ireland were overtaken in August 1914 by the outbreak of the First World War. Both sides agreed to a truce until hostilities ceased, but in April 1916 events in Ireland took a different turn.

An organisation called Sinn Féin (Ourselves Alone) saw an opportunity to exploit the weakness of the Regular British Army while they were engaged in some of the fiercest fighting of the war on the Western Front.

Sir Roger Casement, a Republican sympathiser who had worked as a diplomat for the British Government, went to Germany in the winter of 1914/15 to gain support for the Republican cause. He managed to persuade 55 Irish POW's from the British Army to defect and a shipment of arms was secured from the German Kaiser's government. The men and arms were shipped to Tralee Bay in a Norwegian trawler. The trawler was scuttled by its captain after being challenged by a British warship. Sir Roger was put ashore from a German U-Boat, he was soon captured and later hanged for treason in 1916.

A few days later the Easter rebellion in Dublin was doomed to failure in military terms, but was a great political success. Sinn Féin declared that they were the 'Provisional Government of the Irish Republic'. The rebellion was soon quashed after a few days when British reinforcements were called in by Sir John Maxwell, the local commander, who believed that the Germans were behind the intended coup.

Stringent measures were called for by the British to strike fear into the Republicans. 15 of the rebel leaders were found guilty by courts martial and shot for treason. Other leaders, including Eamon de Valera and Michael Collins, were imprisoned. The executed leaders became martyrs to the Republican cause and support of Sinn Féin increased.

THE IRISH 1916 MEDAL

The 1916 medal was mainly awarded to members of the Dublin Brigade of the Irish Republican Army.

DESCRIPTION: Bronze star shaped reproduction of the IRA cap badge with the letters in the centre replaced by a replica in low relief of the statue erected as a 1916 memorial in the Dublin Post Office. The Irish government also awarded a pension in respect of this medal.

RIBBON: Half orange, half green with a chased bar at the top.

VALUATION: £1000 - £3000 for original 1916 medals.

THE IRISH GENERAL SERVICE MEDAL 1917 - 1921

This medal was awarded to all those who took part in the war struggle for secession from British rule. From the Easter Uprising in 1916 to the signing of the treaty resulting in the emergence of the Irish Free State in 1921.

After the executions of the rebels that took part in Dublin Easter Uprising Sinn Féin gained much public support and sympathy. The men who died on hunger strike in prison became an inspiration to the Republican cause. The general feeling among the Nationalists was that they now considered themselves as soldiers fighting a war against Irelands enemy - Britain.

As support for Sinn Féin grew, large areas of the South became ungovernable. Meanwhile Sinn Féin bolstered up its depleted arsenal by stealing weapons from remote farms and country houses. The intimidation of the Royal Irish Constabulary (RIC) began in earnest resulting in some areas coming under direct British military control.

The British government, partly looking for American participation in the war in Europe, and partly to ease tension for the Irish Convention, began to release the remaining prisoners that had taken part in the Uprising.

The heroes of the rebellion put their signatures to an address to US President Wilson and the American Congress stating their rights to 'defend themselves against external aggression and influence'. This declaration by the Republicans was seen as the commencement of war proper.

The Volunteers were now seen in the open as a uniformed military unit, for example they were on guard at de Valera's election victory in East Clare. De Valera and Michael Collins gradually gained control of the Volunteers, the IRB (Irish Republican Brotherhood, soon to become the IRA), and Sinn Féin.

In 1917, as the war raged in Europe, the question of conscription of Irishmen into British forces came to the forefront. Conscription had already been introduced in Great Britain. Sinn Féin, at this time, was engaged in 'cattle rustling' - stopping animals destined to feed British troops on the front line, from being exported to France.

By the spring of 1918 the (British) Irish Cabinet Commitee had drawn up a blueprint for a Home Rule Bill that would give Ireland 'Dominion Status' in line with other countries such as Australia, New Zealand and Canada. The Bill was not acceptable to Dublin or the Unionists of Ulster. Some members of the British Government saw partition as the only logical answer. The British Government was also trying to bring in the Conscription Bill; the Nationalists saw this as a 'declaration of war'. Luckily for all concerned the Great War ended before the Conscription Bill became law, and it was cancelled.

In 1918 Field Marshal Lord French, the first leader of the BEF (British Expeditionary Force) in France and Belgium, became Lord Lieutenant and Governor General of Ireland. French saw the whole Nationalist and Sinn Féin ambitions as part of the German plot to undermine the British in Ireland. In truth though, the Germans had more important issues to address.

THE IRISH GENERAL SERVICE MEDAL 1917 - 1921

The Field Marshal was preparing for hostile action as the Defence of the Realm Act was applied to prohibit militaristic displays by the Nationalists and Volunteers. The armistice had removed the conscription question, the Home Rule problem still had to be addressed. The general election of 14 December 1918 saw Sinn Féin winning 73 out of 105 seats. Sinn Féin now wanted an all Ireland Republic totally independent from Britain. At the first meeting of the Dáil in Dublin, January 1919, there was a formal declaration for an Irish Republic and a demand for a general withdrawal of British troops from Ireland.

The start of violence began when two RUC officers, guarding a load of gelignite in Tipperary, were shot and killed by Volunteers (now to be known as the Irish Republican Army). Suspects were rounded up and jailed under the Defence of the Realm Act.

The IRA copied the tactics of the Boers 20 years earlier in South Africa, for their guerrilla warfare between 1919 and 1920. Not only were they attacking the RUC, the British Army and the Royal Air Force, there was also intimidation of people who worked at any British military establishment and even at Coastguard stations.

DESCRIPTION: An armed soldier standing in the centre with four crests and the word 'Éire' surrounding him.

RIBBON: Equal stripes of black and orange.

VALUATION: £250 - £350

THE EMERGENCY SERVICE MEDAL 1939 - 1946

The Irish Free State, or Éire as it was known from 1937, declared itself neutral during the Second World War. Despite that, the Dublin Government took defensive contingency measures during this period, which became known as 'The Emergency'.

Under the terms of the 1921 Anglo-Irish Treaty a number of ports were retained under British control. In April 1937 an agreement was reached between the British Government under Neville Chamberlain to return the ports to Irish control, allowing the Irish Government to be seen to be neutral, although technically still a commonwealth member.

Before WWII the Irish Forces consisted of four Gloucester Gladiator fighter planes, six Hawker Hind trainers, a few Walrus sea planes, two ex Royal Navy patrol boats and two torpedo boats. The army had been reduced, to save tax payers money, to about 4,000 men. In twelve months the Irish Armed forces were increased to approximately 50,000 men. In addition other organisations, such as the Air Raid Precaution Service (ARPS) and the Voluntary Aid Division of the Irish Red Cross were formed.

Although officially neutral there was a certain amount of covert co-operation between Ireland and its British neighbour during the war. For example, RAF pilots were repatriated back to Britain and there was intelligence sharing going on. Irish citizens were free to enlist in British forces or to work in British factories.

During WWII there were a number of German bombing incidents in Ireland, mostly in Belfast where there were 740 fatalities. 88 people were killed in Eire and in 1958 the German government paid £327,000 to the Irish republic in reparations.

This medal was instituted 6th October 1944 for Defence Service Personnel who had served with good conduct between 3rd September 1939 and 31st March 1946. The qualifying period was one year for the Defence Forces (and reserves), the Army Nursing Service, the Chaplaincy Service and the Local Defence Forces. For the Local Security Force, the Air Raid Precautions Service and the Irish Red Cross Society the qualifying period was two years

DESCRIPTION: Obverse - A female figure with sword and Irish Wolf Hound at her side. Around the upper of the medal are the Gaelic words RÉ NA PRÁINNE (Emergency period). Reverse - A laurel spray between the dates 1939 and 1946, above which is the title of the unit in which the recipient served (there are 11 in all). The top bar brooch has the wording SEIRBHIS NÁIÚNTA (National Service). For a further two years service a bronze bar was added with a laurel spray design.

RIBBON: Usually reddish-orange with two white centre stripes. Some were issued with a single white centre stripe.

VALUATION: About £35 - £60 for the commoner types, which include those awarded to The Defence Force, The Local Defence Force, Second Line Volunteer Reserve, Army Nursing Service, Air Raids Precautions Organisations and Local Security Force. Approximate values for the less common types are as follows:

26th Battalion (Old IRA soldiers that took part in the 1916 rising) £250
Maritime Inscription (Second line Naval Reserve) £200
Chaplaincy Service - Excessively Rare
Volunteer Aid - Irish Red Cross society £80
First Aid - Irish Red Cross society £80

THE EMERGENCY SERVICE MEDAL 1939 - 1946

The Irish Emergency service medal - This example was awarded to a member of the local security force.

THE MERCHANT SERVICE MEDAL 1939 - 1946

Instituted in 1944 for six months' continous service between September 1939 and March 1946 on Irish registered merchant ships. An extra bar was awarded for every two years in excess of the initial six month period.

During the Second World War the general population of Éire suffered the same hardships as the people in Great Britain were enduring. There was disruption to normal shipping throughout the war and the Irish Government also had to introduce rationing.

Among the goods rationed were petrol, coal, tea and bread. Arable land was increased from 1.5 million acres to 2.5 million acres. To make matters worse, the British enforced a 'navicert' or warrant system, whereby Irish ships had to first dock at British ports for inspection before every voyage and would have to run the danger of U-boat attacks and the extra expense of many extra nautical miles to each journey.

In total 20, mainly smaller Irish ships were lost during the war including two American ships on loan.

DESCRIPTION: Obverse - Same as the Emergency Service Medal - A female figure with sword and Irish Wolf Hound at her side. Around the upper of the medal are the Gaelic words RÉ NA PRÁINNE (Emergency period). Reverse - A steam ship in the foreground with a sailing ship on the horizon. Date 1939 - 1946 shown below, and above, the words 'AN TSEIRBHIS MHUIR - TRÁCTALÁ' (The Merchant Marine Service). For a further two years' service a bronze bar was added with a laurel spray design.

RIBBON: Blue with a centre stripe of white.

VALUATION: £600 - £800

(It is estimated that only 508 of these medals were awarded. 287 without bars, 127 with one, 37 with two bars and 57 with three).

THE IRISH MERCHANT SERVICE MEDAL 1939 - 1946

THE PERMANENT DEFENCE FORCES SERVICE MEDAL

Instituted in September 1944 to be awarded to members of the Defence Forces below commissioned rank for ten years service with good conduct. A bar was added for a further five years service.

DESCRIPTION: Obverse - Female figure of Éire placing a wreath on a kneeling soldier. On the left, the wording 'AN BONN SERBHISE'. Reverse - In English: 'THE SERVICE MEDAL' The medal also has the recipient's name and service number inscribed onto it. The top bar brooch has the word 'SEIRBHIS' on it.

METAL: A Bronze alloy

RIBBON: Usually St. Patrick's blue. When the five year bar is added the ribbon is changed to a blue one with a golden yellow central stripe.

VALUATION: £50 - £80 (or £100 - £120 with extra 5 year bar. The bar has an image of a cross flanked by laurel sprays)

ÉIRE UNITED NATIONS MEDAL AWARDS

The UN Medal is a standard design with various different ribbon colours. Some medals have a clasp.

DESCRIPTION: Obverse - A Wreathed globe with the letters 'UN' at the top. Reverse - The wording 'IN THE SERVICE OF PEACE'.

UN Observation Group in Lebanon (UNOGIL) 1958
RIBBON: Blue with two narrow stripes near the edges.

Organisation des Nations Unies au Congo (ONUC) 1960 - 1964
RIBBON: As above with clasp 'CONGO'.

UN Force in Cyprus (UNFICYP) 1964 onwards
RIBBON: Pale blue with central white stripe bordered by two dark blue stripes. See page 72.

UN Interim Force in Lebanon (UNIFIL) 1978 onwards
RIBBON: Pale blue with green centre bordered by white and red.

UN Mission in Kosovo (UNMIK) 1999 onwards
RIBBON: Pale blue with a wide central dark blue stripe edged with white.

VALUATIONS: All £18 - £22, except original striking for Cyprus, £30 - £35.

Appendix I - Researching

Named medals, for example, all First World War medals are engraved on the lower rim with the recipient's name, rank, number and regiment or ship. In the case of the World War I Stars these details will be seen on the plain back of the medal. An example of the name wording would be something like this:

PO 14544, PTE B. T. RITTY, R.M.L.I (Royal Marine Light Infantry Division).

From these details it's possible to do further research on Private B T Ritty, by obtaining his service record and other medal awards by going to the Public Record Office at Kew in London (www.pro.gov.uk).

For research from World War II onwards:

British Army (including ATS)
Army Personnel Centre
Historic Disclosures
65 Brown St.
Glasgow
G2 8EX
SCOTLAND

Royal Navy (including WRNS) for Officers still serving or retired under age 60:

Naval Secretary
Victory Building
HM Naval Base,
Portsmouth,
Hampshire,
PO1 3LS
ENGLAND

Other ranks who enlisted before 2 Sep 1939 & officers who enlisted before 1950:

Royal Naval Records
DR2A Navy Search
Bourne Ave.,
Hayes, Middlesex
UB3 1RF
ENGLAND

Other ranks who enlisted after 3 Sep 1939:

Naval Pay & Pensions
HMS Centurion
Grange Road,
Gosport, Hampshire,
PO13 9XA
ENGLAND

Royal Marines:

Royal Marines Historical Record Office,
HMS Centurion
Address as above.

Appendix I - Researching

Royal Air Force:

Officers- PMA(CS)2a(2)a,
RAF Innsworth
Gloucester,
GL3 1EZ

Please note that some of the organisations listed on these pages will only give out information or engage in medal claims for family or next of kin.

The Royal British Legion (www.britishlegion.org.uk) and Forces Reunited (www.forcesreunited.org.uk) can also be good sources of information.

For details of WWII Veterans' Medal entitlements:

Armed Forces Personnel Administration Agency
M.O.D. Medal Office,
Building 250,
RAF Innswoth,
Gloucester,
GL3 1EZ
ENGLAND

The names of Privates E Cleaver and J Last can be seen on these WWI medals.

Selected Further Reading

The Boer War, Field Marshal Lord Carver, Pan/National Army Museum (2000). ISBN: 033036944X

The First World War, John Keegan, Pimlico (1999). ISBN: 0712666451

1918 - Year of Victory, Malcolm Brown, Imperial War Museum/Pan Books (1999). ISBN: 0330376721

The Royal Marines, Major-General J.L. Moulton, Royal Marines Museum. ISBN: 0950523526

Intervention in Russia 1918-1920, Miles Hudson, Leo Cooper Ltd (2004). ISBN: 184415033X

Engage The Enemy More Closely, Correlli Barnett, Penguin Books (2000). ISBN: 0141390085

Why The Allies Won, Richard Overy, Pimlico. The new 2006 edition, due to be published August 2006 will have ISBN: 1845950658

The Korean War, Max Hastings, Pan Books. ISBN: 0330392883

The Falklands War, P. Eddy, M. Linklater & P. Gillman, Andre Deutsch.

Who Dares Wins (the story of the SAS 1950 - 1992), Tony Geraghty, Abacus (2002). ISBN 0349114870

Collecting Medals and Decorations, Alec A. Purves, B.A. Seaby (later editions published by Spink & Son). ISBN: (1978 edition) 0900652454

The Medals, Decorations & Orders of the Great War 1914-1918, Alec A. Purves, Savannah Publications (1989). ISBN 090375438X

The Medals, Decorations & Orders of the 2nd World War 1939-1945, Alec A. Purves, Savannah Publications (2004). ISBN 1902366352

Ireland in the 20th Century, Tim Pat Coogan, Arrow Books (2004). ISBN: 0099415224

A Guide to Military Museums, Terence Wise 1994 (editor and publisher). ISBN: 185674020X